The Wedding Planning

Survive the Stress, Stay Sane, & Pl:

Christian Seg:

Copyright © 2019 Christian Segarra
All rights reserved

Table of Contents

Table of Contents	3
A Special Shout-Out	6
A Small Favor	7
So, You're Getting Married? Congratulations! Here's Why You Should Read This Book	8
Pick a Wedding Date That Your Savings Account Won't Hate	11
The 5 Crucial Steps That Will Keep Your Wedding Personal and Costs under Control	15
Pick an Awesome Venue by Following These 5 Simple Steps	19
Not All Vendors Are Created Equal. Spend Your Money Where it Matters	26
• Photographer: Look like a Royal, Not a Hobbit	29
• DJ & MC: "Wow! Your Music Really Sucked, but the Wedding was Still Great!" Said No Wedding Guest Ever	37
• Florist & Decorator: Nobody Will Remember the Flowers	40
• Officiant & Place of Worship: Why this is Make or Break	49
• The Catholic Wedding: The Unexpected Penance We Had to Endure	54
• Wedding Limo & Other Transportation: All That Matters is That You Get There	62
• Hey, We're Finally Done With Vendors – Just Kidding Here's Some More Advice	67

- Payments Schedule: Why You Should Absolutely Pay Attention to This 69

Finally, Some Downtime. Here's How to Effectively Utilize It 72

- Wedding Dress: To Rent, Or Not To Rent, That Is the Question 74
- Wedding Party Outfits: Your Bridesmaids and Groomsmen Should Dress to Impress, but You Should Be the Stars of the Show 77
- Wedding Bands: A Cautionary Tale 80
- Honeymoon: Start Planning Sooner Rather Than Later 84
- Bachelor/Bachelorette Party: Enjoy Your Party, But Don't Bite Off More Than You Can Chew 86
- Save-the-Dates & Wedding Invitations: The When and Where is Important – The Paper It's Printed On, Less So 88
- Deal Hunting & Cost Cutting: Save Now, Reap the Benefits Later 91

A Breakdown of All the Small Details You Need to Finalize & How Not To Lose Your Mind 94

- Venue: Select From the Defaults, Save Time & Money 95
- Photographer: Just Tell Them Where to Show Up 99
- DJ: Choose Your Tunes, but Keep Your Audience in Mind 100
- Florist/Decorator: The Flor(ist) is Lava! Don't Burn All of Your Cash on Flowers 102

- Catholic Church: Thou Shall... Confirm Logistics with the Priest   104
- Wedding Programs: The Perfect Way to Engage Your Guests... For All of Two Minutes   106
- Rehearsal Dinner: If You Wait Too Long to Make a Reservation, Your Only Option May End up Being the McDonald's Drive-Thru   108
- Legal Requirements   111
- Some Minor Things to Remember   112

Your Special Day Is Here... Some Advice   115

And They Lived Happily Ever After   120

Thank You for Reading! Please Share Your Feedback   125

About the Author   126

So, You're Getting Married? Congratulations! Here's Why You Should Read This Book

Planning a wedding can be a very stressful and costly endeavor. The stress and costs are why roughly 30% of couples getting married opt to hire a wedding planner or day-of coordinator to handle some or all aspects of their wedding. Wedding planners, however, are not cheap. You can expect to pay anywhere between $500 and $1,500 for a day-of wedding coordinator, and as much as $3,000 - $8,000 for a full-service wedding planner to handle the details from beginning to end.

Weddings are pricey enough on their own, and many people would like to avoid the additional cost of a wedding planner, if possible. Fortunately, this book aims to show you that with enough planning, thought, and preparation, you and your significant other can plan your wedding while minimizing the gray hairs that come from doing so and still make it the most special day of your life.

The Inspiration for Writing This Book

When my wife and I first became engaged, we were ecstatic at the thought of getting married. However, this quickly turned to anxiety when we realized how many things we had to take care of while also trying to keep costs reasonable, given that we were paying for the wedding ourselves. We did as much research as we could online, but to be frank, many of the wedding blogs either did not go into as much detail as we would have liked or only covered certain aspects of wedding planning. Some other blogs, which I will not mention, just didn't keep it real. If those blogs were all you ever read, you would think that planning a wedding was an incredibly simple, stress-free process, and maybe for those with an unlimited budget, it is.

However, I am going to assume that if you are reading this book, it's because you want to try to have as beautiful of a wedding as possible without having to consign yourself to indentured servitude. With that in mind, my wife and I thought it would be a great idea to share our experience in as much detail as possible, as well as give some honest advice so that you and others can benefit from it while planning your wedding.

What Nobody Tells You About Wedding Planning

One of the things my wife and I realized pretty early on was how little transparency there was into venue and vendor pricing. The lack of transparency made it very difficult to tell whether we were getting a fair price or not. I'm sure most of you will agree that nobody likes walking out of a meeting feeling like they just got ripped off. We also could never have guessed how many small details we needed to decide upon at the last minute.

That's why in this book we will go through the whole wedding process from the minute you put a ring on it, to last call at your reception. We will speak mainly from personal experience, but will also include advice based on what some of our friends experienced, as well as other research we have done. We will be as detailed as possible and will even include what we paid for vendors and our thought process on some of the decisions we made.

Quick Disclaimer

Please note that the prices I will share were locked in over a year before our wedding. Pricing obtained closer in than a year out may be higher. Additionally, we were married in 2018, so all of the prices I will provide were quoted to us in 2017. Pricing may change over time, but we hope the quotes we share will still be helpful to you in establishing some kind of baseline.

Remember This Crucial Fact

Now, I must emphasize that planning ahead is KEY to minimizing stress and having more CONTROL over your costs. I highly recommend giving yourself at least one year before your wedding. I know the feeling of just getting engaged and wanting to get married tomorrow, but trying to plan a wedding in such a short time will be stressful, and your options for booking a venue, photographer, or DJ will be limited. The majority of couples book their wedding venue at least one year in advance, but often even sooner than that. Couples do this because they want to reserve the desirable locations while they're still available. Keep in mind some of the fancy venues can get booked two or more years in advance.

So, if you get engaged and want to plan a wedding in six months, be prepared to have fewer venues and vendors available. Those that are available may try to charge you a higher price, given that you are on a tighter timeline. For those of you that are feeling brave and want to start planning a wedding for next month, be prepared to accept that the only venue available might be Chuck E. Cheese. We discuss venues and vendors later, but for now, let's get started!

Pick a Wedding Date That Your Savings Account Won't Hate

First things first, you need to pick a date for your wedding, preferably not by throwing a dart at a calendar. You may already have a specific date in mind that has some personal significance, such as your anniversary date, or the date you first met, etc. However, it is crucial to keep in mind how the time of year, day of the week, and time of day can affect your wedding costs.

Time of Year

The month you choose for your wedding can have a significant impact on costs. Peak wedding months can vary depending on the climate of where you live, but in general, wedding season in the United States is from May through October, with peaks occurring in June & September. Expect to pay as much as 30% more for your venue during this period when compared to the off-peak. Vendors also tend to be more expensive during this period and get booked out farther in advance – especially the good ones.

Some exceptions to this are:

1. Ski season at ski towns: Months that are typically off-peak will not be off-peak during ski season. Expect peak prices.
2. Summer in the American South: While the summer months are usually peak season, they may not necessarily be peak season in the South, especially if you're thinking about an outdoor wedding. Temperatures can regularly reach the triple digits. Add in a good dose of humidity and mosquitos, and you get bad hair days, soaked tuxedos, itchy legs, and possibly your guests cursing you under their breath for making them endure that.

3. Holidays & Special Events: Christmas and Valentine's Day will most definitely 100% be priced for peak demand. The 2nd half of December, in general, may see higher pricing due to corporate holiday parties.

Day of Week

The day of the week you schedule your wedding can also significantly affect your costs. It may not come as a surprise that Saturday is the most popular day for a wedding. Guests tend to generally be available and not have any work conflicts on Saturdays, which means nobody needs to take a day off from work to attend your wedding. Additionally, your guests will surely appreciate having Sunday as a recovery day for any hangovers or lengthy travel times. All of these factors add up to Saturday being the most in-demand day of the week for a wedding, and consequently, the most expensive.

Sunday is the second most popular day. Like Saturday, guests tend not to have any work-related conflicts on Sundays. However, most people's workweek starts on Monday, which makes the day slightly inconvenient, especially if you are traveling from far away.

Weekdays tend to be the cheapest days of the week to get married, especially Tuesday or Wednesday. A weekday wedding may require your guests to take at least one day off during the middle of the week with possibly no recovery day. For this reason, weekday weddings are typically in low demand and are priced to reflect that. Corporate events such as exhibitions, cocktail hours, or networking sessions are an exception to this. Since companies tend to host events during the week, they will be who you are competing against for scheduling.

If you are thinking about a weekday wedding, it may be helpful to make sure there aren't any major conventions or corporate gatherings happening around your area. However, if you and the majority of your guests work a typical Monday through Friday schedule, there really is no reason to schedule your wedding on a weekday. Although doing so might be an excellent way to get people who you felt obligated to invite to your wedding, but didn't actually want them to come, to not show up.

Time of Day

The last time-related factor that will affect your wedding costs is the time of day. Most venues will give you the option for an afternoon (12PM – 5PM) or an evening wedding (6PM – 11PM). Daytime weddings are cheaper than evening weddings. The price difference makes sense for a weekday since those guests that choose not to take the day off can still leave work a little bit early to make it to your wedding. However, even weekend weddings are cheaper during the day than in the evening. For example, my wife and I chose Saturday afternoon for our wedding. Had we chosen Saturday evening, the cost of our venue would have almost doubled.

Another factor that I have not discussed yet is guest minimums. Peak Season/Day of Week/Time of Day has stricter requirements for guest minimums than off-peak. For example, the guest minimum for our Saturday afternoon wedding was 100 guests. Had we chosen Saturday evening, our guest minimum would have increased to 150 guests. That's an extra 50 guests that I would have had to pay for to secure the evening slot, even if I didn't have an additional 50 people I wanted to invite! We will discuss this in more detail in the venue section.

Keep all of these factors in mind when you choose your date. The time of day decision doesn't need to be made right away, but it's still worth keeping in the back of your mind.

The 5 Crucial Steps That Will Keep Your Wedding Personal and Costs under Control

Now that you have a wedding date in mind, it's time for one of the tougher steps: the guest list. The number of people you want to invite will influence what venues you will look at because many of them have guest minimums or maximums. Your guest list will also determine what style of wedding is even possible. After all, it's difficult to have an intimate garden-style wedding when you plan to invite 200 people. I've outlined five steps to help you build a guest list that should keep costs down and keep your special day as intimate as possible.

Step 1: Write Down Literally Everybody That Comes to Mind

There will be many people you will want to invite to your wedding, especially while you are still basking in that engagement glow. However, it is important to remember that inviting one person may require you to invite somebody else too. As you are writing down the people you are considering inviting to the wedding, remember to include spouses, significant others, children, etc. After all, it may come off as a little odd or rude for you to invite your cousin, but not her husband or kids.

Step 2: Identify Your Must-Haves

Next, you should categorize every person on your tentative guest list into two categories:

1. Must-Haves
2. Nice-to-Haves

The Must-Haves should be made up of people that you would be absolutely heartbroken and borderline offended if they did not attend.

For example, if my brother told me that he would not be able to attend my wedding because he had already planned a vacation, I would have phoned an anonymous tip to TSA accusing him of being a terrorist so that he ended up on a no-fly list. This would have effectively canceled his vacation and left him no choice but to attend my wedding. Okay, this is obviously an exaggeration, but the point is you would really want this person at your wedding.

The Nice-to-Haves should be made up of people that you would like to have at your wedding, but would be understanding and forgiving if something came up and they could not make it. For example, one of my wife's friends had intended to come to the wedding, but then couldn't make it because they waited a little too long to book their flight, and by the time they did bother to check flights, tickets were well over $1,000. While this annoyed my wife, it didn't induce the burning rage that I have seen her capable of, and ultimately, she got over it.

Step 3: Categorize Your Nice-to-Haves as a Friend or Family Member

Now, everybody's situation is different, but in general, family tends to be non-negotiable. Your relatives' spouses and children also tend to be non-negotiable. For those of you who have large families as my wife does, you will find that your guest list is probably already at a high count, and you haven't even started counting friends yet.

You probably don't need to invite every single cousin, unless you grew up together and are very close, but keep in mind that if the guest list needs to be trimmed down, it will probably be people from the "friends" subcategory that will be cut. Of course, if you don't mind your entire family asking for all of eternity why you invited that one friend you talk to twice a year but didn't invite your cousin Brenda, then feel free to trim from the family subcategory.

Step 4: Casually Let Your Must-Haves Know What Time Frame You're Thinking

Next on the list is to let your Must-Haves know what timeframe you're thinking of for your wedding. The timeframe you communicate could be an actual date, or it could be more general, like July 2020 or even Summer 2020. I know some of you might be thinking that it is way too soon to do this and that this is what the save-the-dates or invitations are supposed to communicate. Let me clarify.

The purpose of casually reaching out this early on is not to get a definite "yes" or "no". The goal is to let your Must-Haves know that you are thinking about a specific date, and you wanted to make sure that they don't already have something planned because you really want them to be able to make it. When you take this approach, three things can happen:

1. It turns out that somebody you want at your wedding has some other obligation that they cannot get out of. You now have the flexibility to consider a different date.
2. It turns out that somebody you want at your wedding has some other obligation that they cannot get out of. You decide to keep the date the same and accept that this person will not make it to your wedding.
3. The person has no conflicts and will have no problem attending, as of that point in time.

Regardless of which of these three scenarios occur, you now have more data on which to build your preliminary guest list, which will, in turn, be used to decide on a venue. Repeat after me: MORE DATA IS GOOD.

If you wait until your save-the-dates go out to communicate your wedding date, you run the risk of people planning something during that time, such as a vacation or other event. This could result in in my experience. You will likely have to go in-person to find out pricing and possibly negotiate from there.

Step 2: Create a List of Venues You Are Interested In

After looking through as many venues as you have the patience for, make a list of the ones you like most. If there is a venue you are interested in that has a maximum guest count listed, you will have to cross-check this with your initial guest tally to make sure that the venue can hold all of your guests, unless you really like that venue and are willing to unfriend some folks. Otherwise, I recommend having at least four venues on your list.

Step 3: Visit the Venues on Your List in-Person

Next, you will need to visit all of the venues on your shortlist. You should call to set up an appointment to meet with a banquet manager. They will show you around the venue and then sit you down to discuss pricing. The price they will quote to you will vary by what month, day of the week, and time of day your wedding date is, as discussed previously. They will ask how many people you will be expecting at your wedding because most venues will require a minimum guest guarantee. Depending on the venue, they may have several ballrooms, each with varying minimum guest counts. This is where the tentative Must-Have guest count will be useful. Your tentative guest list will help you determine which ballrooms are right for your guest count.

At this point, I think it is important to mention that if the banquet manager starts to get pushy, do not feel obligated to sign a contract on the spot. Here is an example of what I mean:

My wife and I were looking at a venue in New Jersey, and after showing us the venue, the banquet manager wanted us to sign a contract on the spot. The prices the banquet manager was quoting were a little above our price range, and we still had two more venues we were going to look at. We mentioned that we didn't want to sign a contract yet because we still had some more venues to see. The banquet manager ended up replying in a very condescending tone, "well, how many venues do you need to look at?". If this happens to you, I highly recommend that you move on and consider other venues instead. If they are treating you like this before they have your money, just imagine how you will be treated once they already have your money in their pocket.

After pricing is discussed with the banquet manager, you should visit all of the other venues on your list and get price quotes for each venue that you are seriously considering so that you can compare them. Pricing is discussed in more detail in the next step.

Step 4: Compare the Venues

After visiting each venue on your list and obtaining price quotes, you should compare the pros, cons, and costs of each venue. In the New York City area, the price quotes you are given will be the base cost per person. Then, on top of this, taxes and a service charge are added. For example, if you are quoted $100++, this means the cost of the venue will be $100 per person, plus taxes, plus a service charge, typically 20% in the New York City area. You will also be expected to tip on top of this. The tip will most certainly vary by venue. Here I'll provide some background on our experience with pricing.

My wife and I were married in Queens, New York City. The venue we ended up choosing quoted us $70++ for a Saturday afternoon wedding in October. After taxes and the service charge, this ended up totaling approximately $92 per person (children were half price, infants were free). On top of this, the venue communicated to us that we were expected to tip $4 per person, bring our final cost per person to $96. Included in this price were the open bar, hors d'oeuvres, a carving station (which we negotiated), six buffet-style entrees of our choice for the cocktail hour, the actual sit-down dinner, dessert table, and a four-tier wedding cake.

Had we chosen a Saturday evening wedding, the cost per person would have increased to $120++ for the same items. In general, I would not say we are expert negotiators. Still, it seemed that a few dollars off the price per person or an extra station, such as a carving station or fondue station, were the limit to how much negotiation could get you.

We looked at other venues as well in Long Island and New Jersey for the same day of week and time of day. The least expensive place we found in Long Island quoted us $85++, while the cheapest place in New Jersey (outside of Newark) we found quoted us $120++. We initially looked outside of New York City because we thought we could get a better deal. However, the opposite was true. I suspect banquet halls in New York City (excluding Manhattan) ended up being priced lower because there was a more abundant supply of banquet halls to compete with. This may be something to keep in mind when searching for venues.

As a final note for this section, I highly recommend looking at totals instead of cost per person. $120++ per person may not sound too high at first, but when you multiply this by the number of your Must-Haves, you will get a much clearer idea of the costs. For example, many people consider a 100-person wedding to be small. However, at a rate of $120++ per person in New York City, this 100-person wedding will end up costing over $15,000. Keep in mind this is only the cost of your venue. Your DJ, photographer, florist, and other vendors will all be additional costs.

If you're paying for the wedding yourself, this realization can seem daunting. It certainly made me shit myself. The good news is that the venue is the most expensive vendor. The other vendors, such as DJ or florist, should be less costly unless you decide to make your wedding akin to that of the old Roman emperors. However, if that is your goal, this is probably not the book for you.

Step 5: Sign Contract with Venue

Once you have compared all of the pros, cons, and pricing for each venue, you can finally choose the one you think suits your needs best. Once you have selected your preferred venue, you will need to meet with the banquet manager once again to sign the contract. The contract will indicate the agreed-upon rate per person, the minimum guest count, and any items included in the rate. Make 100% sure that everything is clearly spelled out in the contract. I cannot emphasize this enough.

If you negotiated an extra station, such as a carving station, but see that it's not explicitly spelled out in the contract, do not be surprised if come wedding day, the carving station is nowhere to be seen. DO NOT take the banquet manager's word that they will remember when the time comes. Make sure your contract is crystal clear. After you sign the agreement, be sure to make several copies and store them in different places. If ever there is a dispute on what was agreed upon, you want to make sure you have your contract handy.

Our Venue Experience

Overall, we had a great experience with our venue. The banquet manager we met with for the initial meeting made us feel very comfortable and didn't try so obviously hard to sell us. He let the

Not All Vendors Are Created Equal. Spend Your Money Where it Matters

So, you've picked your venue. Great! Now you have to choose your vendors. Technically, you can hire as many vendors as you want for whatever detail you want them to handle. However, we will discuss only the ones that I think are the most important. They are:

1. Photographer
2. DJ
3. Florist/Decorator
4. Church/Officiant
5. Transportation (limo, driver, vintage car rental, etc.)

Some venues may provide you with a list of vendors that they have a good working relationship with, as our venue did. They reasoned that these vendors knew the venue very well and were reliable. While I'm sure there was some referral scheme going on, I will admit that logically, they had a point. If your venue has a list of preferred vendors, it definitely makes a good starting point. However, do not at all feel obligated to choose any of those vendors.

In this section, I'll provide my thoughts on the importance of each of these vendors, what criteria we looked for, and what my wife and I ended up booking. In general, the same steps we provided for choosing an excellent venue can also be used for selecting high-caliber vendors, with some minor tweaks. These steps are:

1. Search for vendors on the internet or start with the list of preferred vendors that your venue gives you.
2. After looking at photos, reviews, and portfolios, make a list of the vendors that you are interested in.

3. Set up in-person meetings with the vendors to find out the pricing for the products they are offering, and to see how comfortable they make you feel.
4. Compare your experience, products, and pricing from each vendor to see which ones you would prefer. If possible, try to negotiate a price match if one vendor offers lower pricing than a competitor does.
5. Sign the contract with your vendor, but ensure that all of the items you are purchasing, prices, and payment schedules are explicitly spelled out in the contract.

You may see me mention these steps again for emphasis throughout this section. Now, before moving on to discuss each vendor, I want to preemptively address what is sometimes referred to as the wedding tax.

The Wedding Tax

Many individuals believe from their experiences that the vendor will charge higher prices once you tell them that your event is a wedding and that this is why they always begin their meeting by asking what kind of event you are planning. I do not have any concrete evidence to support this, but I am also of the same opinion. I've done some reading since my wedding, and my initial opinion before researching the topic more in-depth was that these vendors were taking advantage of engaged couples.

However, I have since learned that weddings are two levels of stress greater than any other event. There is much less room for error, as the wedding couple will not tolerate any screw-ups, even if they happen to be out of the vendor's control. To make sure that there aren't any screw-ups, vendors typically have to take on extra material, labor, and planning costs. In addition to this, they also seem to compensate themselves for the shortened lifespan that comes with being in charge of other people's weddings. So definitely expect higher prices versus what you would see for any other event, but maybe accept that there is a reason for that.

With all that being said, let's discuss our first vendor.

Photographer: Look like a Royal, Not a Hobbit

I think if you are going to spend some extra money, this is one of the places to do it. You are going to be looking at these pictures for years to come, and there are no do-overs, so you most certainly want to make sure you hire a quality photographer. Now, there are three ways you can go about getting a photographer. You can:

1. Contract directly with the photographer
2. Hire a studio that provides a photographer
3. Ask all of your wedding guests to take pictures on their phones throughout the day and select your favorites at the end

I half-jokingly brought up option three as a possibility to my wife. Let me tell you if looks could kill, I'd be six feet under right now. So let's just focus on options 1 and 2. Both approaches will have their pros and cons. Let's start with the studio first.

Obtaining a Photographer through a Studio

The main advantage of booking a photographer through a studio is that by booking with them, you are also gaining access to their resources. Studios typically will:

- Have several photographers on call that they can dispatch to events in case the scheduled photographer has an emergency. They can even dispatch several photographers for the same event.
- Act as a one-stop-shop by producing and editing all of your photos, creating your photo album, and providing other extras such as photo booths.
- Offer you better value since they can offer bundle packages.

However, the studio's most significant strength can also be their biggest downside. For example, the studio may have access to an ample supply of photographers, but these photographers are typically contractors, not permanent employees. They are free to go as they please. Sure, some photographers might have an excellent working relationship with a studio and stick around with that studio for a long time. Still, there is always the chance that they will leave the studio or that the studio will end their working relationship. This is a disadvantage because:

- Picking a photographer from the studio a year in advance is unrealistic. The chances that the particular photographer you want will still be there on the day of your event is low.
- You may end up with whoever the studio has available on the day of your event. This means you will not be able to meet the photographer in person to see if you like them or not.

Since you probably won't be able to make a judgment call on the photographers themselves, you have to decide whether the studio is good at picking photographers. The key is to judge the studio on their reviews and photo gallery. Do the reviews say their photographers were terrific? Is their photo gallery full of nothing but great pictures? If so, the studio is probably very selective when it comes to photographers. But if you see reviews saying that the photographers are rude or that they missed some important shots, then I think it's best you keep looking.

It also wouldn't hurt to ask the studio how they go about selecting photographers. The owner of the studio we booked with explained to us that in addition to photographic talent, the most important thing he looks for is passion. He said that no matter how good a photographer's photos have been in the past, if they are beginning to lose their passion, he will end their working relationship.

He reasoned that without passion, they will not be able to connect with the wedding couple and may take subpar photos, which will ultimately damage the studio's reputation. This made a lot of sense to me because I doubt anybody wants to be assigned a photographer that looks like they would rather throw themselves into traffic than take another photo of you.

Booking with the Photographer Directly

The biggest advantage of booking directly with a photographer is that you know who you're getting. You can:

- Look at the photographer's portfolio and decide whether you like their pictures or not.
- Meet with them in person and decide whether they are going to be able to make you smile when you're completely stressed out on your wedding day.
- Read reviews and know that they were written about them and not a different photographer, as might be the case with a studio.

We actually met with a photographer from our venue's preferred vendors list that used this as his sales pitch. Logically it made sense, and his pricing wasn't terrible even though his pictures didn't amaze us. However, when we mentioned we still wanted to meet with other studios, he, just like the condescending salesperson from the venue in New Jersey, asked what we needed to meet with them for. Red flag. Since we didn't like the actual photographer, we certainly were not going to book with them, and as a result, their own sales pitch ended up doing them in.

The main downside of contracting directly with the photographer is that they may not have enough resources to act as a one-stop-shop.

- Some photographers might have a fantastic portfolio but will not create an album or prints.
- Others might offer an album, but outsource it to a third party, passing the cost on to you, usually at a worse rate than a studio might offer.
- Even if you find a photographer that has a great portfolio and also edits as well as produces your photos, they may not have availability for your wedding date.
- If the photographer ends up having an emergency the day of your wedding, either you will have no photographer, or you will have an emergency backup photographer that you have never met before, making it no different than booking with a studio.

Our Pricing

Thinking about the pros and cons discussed, you can decide which option suits you best. My wife and I ended up booking a bundled DJ and photography package through a studio because we thought it provided the best value. Our combined DJ and photography package cost $6,000 after taxes. The photography portion accounted for $2,800 of the total and included:

- One photographer covering us for 8 hours
- One 12" x 12" wedding album (70 photos – editing included – digital design)
- Six 8" x 10" prints
- Four 5" x 7" prints
- 100 thank you cards
- One 16" x 20" wedding portrait
- One 11" x 14" engagement portrait
- One CD with all of our wedding photos (not high-resolution)

Our Experience

We met with our photographer for the first time on the morning of our wedding. He was very nice, committed, and enthusiastic about his work. He was also willing to help us with whatever we needed. However, he was maybe too focused on taking pictures and not focused enough on making sure we stuck to our itinerary.

Our ceremony ended up starting late because he spent too much time taking pictures of my wife and her bridesmaids at their hotel in the morning. They took the same picture with slightly different poses and angles. I'm sure some brides would appreciate this, but I would have preferred he spent the extra time doing that at our venue.

We got to our venue late and missed most of our cocktail hour because he wanted to take many pictures at the church, even though the reception venue looked a lot nicer. We were told by a few of our guests that he was "very intense" because he interrupted conversations so that he could get us to pose for more photos. However, at the end of the day, he took over 1,000 photos by himself. He worked 8 hours straight on a very fast-paced day with no break for food and still managed to deliver what we thought were high-quality photos.

Overall, we still thought we had a positive experience with the photographer, but there are some lessons you should take away from our experience. They are:

1. Do NOT be afraid to tell your photographer that you don't want to take pictures at a particular location, or that you would rather be on time. They are there to make sure your day is perfect. If you think your time is better spent taking pictures elsewhere, tell them that. After all, you are the one writing their check. I wish my wife and I had done this. We would not have

started our ceremony half an hour late, and we would have made it to our cocktail hour on time and have been able to enjoy it.
2. Don't compare yourself to other people on social media. My wife and I liked the photos when we first saw them. However, my wife likes to compare everything to photos she sees on Instagram. So naturally, she compared our pictures to wedding photos of "social influencers", whose profession is running and monetizing their social media. After making this comparison, she was not 100% satisfied since she has "seen better on other people's Instagram". No shit.

   These influencers, and really just people in general, aren't going to put bad photos of themselves on Instagram. They are only going to put the best. You also don't know how much money was spent on their photographers, how much time was spent on editing, or how many times they had to retake their pictures because they weren't perfect. You have to keep in mind that these influencers base their livelihood on the images and content they put up on social media.

   My recommendation: don't compare yourself to other people on social media. If you objectively like the photos as you are looking at them, then that is all that matters.
3. If you contracted out a studio, talk to them about meeting whatever photographer they are thinking of assigning to you a month before your wedding. It is highly likely they may not have a photographer assigned until the last minute, but it doesn't hurt to try. If they can fulfill your request, you can meet the photographer, talk about what kind of photos you would like to take, and get a feel for whether you would enjoy working with them or not.

4. As mentioned before, see how the studio or photographer treats you in-person and see if they try to pressure you to book right away instead of exploring your options. Confident vendors will have no problem with you exploring your options because they know or believe that you will be back since they are the best out there. Unconfident vendors will question you on why you don't want to book right away and try to pressure you into signing a contract.

A Brief Note on Videography

Studios will typically also offer videography. They will record footage of your event. Either with a handheld camera or a drone of some sort. Some of the fancier videography packages also include a wedding documentary in which the bride and groom give interviews about how they met and fell in love. I have personally seen some of these wedding documentaries, and they can be quite beautiful.

However, my wife and I met on Tinder, so we didn't think that paying an additional $2,000 to go on camera and say "Yes, it was the most romantic swipe right of my entire life" was worth it for us.

While my wife and I did not get a videography package, we do think it could provide value depending on the couple. Maybe you'd like to have your vows filmed or are having your event at some amazing outdoor venue where it makes sense to have video footage. Or perhaps the story of how you met is truly something out of a fairytale. If this is the case for you, then videography might be worth it.

There were other video-related options that we could have purchased, such as renting huge flat-screen TVs to display videos during our wedding. Apparently, some couples do this to show pictures of themselves growing up. However, at $500 per TV, we did not think it was worth it for us, especially since I was a fugly baby with a ginormous, oddly-shaped head.

DJ & MC: "Wow! Your Music Really Sucked, but the Wedding was Still Great!" Said No Wedding Guest Ever

The DJ is another area where it would make sense to invest more of your budget. The job of the DJ and MC is to make sure everybody has fun. It may not seem like an overly complicated job, especially since anybody with a Spotify playlist calls themselves a DJ nowadays.

However, it's one thing to just pre-build a playlist, but it's a totally different thing to be able to read how a crowd is reacting to the music and be able to adjust accordingly. Just think back to the last time you were at a party, and whoever was responsible for the music just didn't know what the hell they were doing. You do not want this to happen at your wedding.

DJs will often bring an MC with them. The MC will be the one making the necessary announcements during the reception, such as when it's time to make speeches, cut the cake, etc. However, an MC should also serve the function of hyping up the crowd and getting them onto the dance floor. Sometimes the wedding guests are shy and need a nudge to get their asses on the dance floor.

A good MC should be able to get the crowd on the dance floor while the DJ keeps them on the dance floor. A bad DJ will see that the crowd is not responding well to a Taylor Swift song and decide that maybe playing five more Taylor Swift songs will win the crowd over, inevitably driving everybody to the open bar where, like a shunned lover, they will drink to forget.

How to Pick a Quality DJ

Choosing a DJ is similar to choosing a photographer. You can contract an independent DJ, or you can hire one through a studio. The pros and cons are mostly the same, and the due diligence you should do (e.g., reading reviews, asking to see videos of events) is also the same. The only thing that might be different is if your wedding guests will be predominantly of one type of ethnic group, such as mainly Indian, Latino, etc. In this case, you may want to look specifically for a DJ that has experience playing those kinds of events, and that has an expansive music library for them.

Our Pricing

As I mentioned before, my wife and I booked a bundled DJ/Photography package through a studio because we thought it provided the best value. Our combined DJ and photography package cost $6,000 after taxes. The DJ portion accounted for $3,200 of the total and included:

- DJ coverage for the duration of the reception & cocktail hour (5 hours)
- MC coverage for the duration of the reception
- One smoke machine
- 100 party favors
- Intelligent light display (colorful moving lights on the dance floor – don't recommend this for a daytime wedding)
- Custom gobo (our initials and wedding date projected onto the floor)
- Photo booth with attendant (customized strips – all guests received a copy)
- Photo booth props
- Scrapbook with all photo booth pictures inside

Our Experience

We met with our DJ a week before the wedding. Our DJ had experience playing Latino & Filipino events, which is precisely what we needed. We discussed what type of music we would like played at our wedding, what the general age group would be, as well as the ethnic make-up of our guests. We wanted to know every last detail of the order of events for the wedding, such as when we would be announced, when the cake would be cut, etc.

Our DJ told us to relax and not worry about it because they would handle everything. I have to admit we were a little worried when he gave us this response. We wanted to make sure we knew exactly when each step was going to occur so that nothing went wrong. However, during the day of the event, they actually did handle everything, and we did not have to worry about anything. They came and grabbed us when they needed to. There were absolutely no hiccups.

Additionally, our guests told us that our DJ played an amazing party and that our MC was great at getting people to dance. All in all, we had nothing but a positive experience with the DJ and their team.

Florist & Decorator: Nobody Will Remember the Flowers

The role of the florist is to make your wedding look beautiful. They can decorate both your ceremony venue and your reception venue, assuming that they are in different locations. These decorations might be comprised of flowers, backdrops, centerpieces, linens, or furniture. The florist will also handle the bride's bouquet, as well as the flowers for the bridesmaids, groomsmen, and parents.

Why You Shouldn't Overspend In This Area

Now, I'm just going to come right out and say it. I don't think this is an area that's worth a lot of investment. There are two reasons for this.

1. I think the wedding tax is particularly extreme here. The mark-up on the flowers and decorations is much more noticeable because a lot of us have bought flowers or have created DIY decorations at some point in our lives, and will notice the price difference.
2. Years after your wedding, it is very likely that most of your wedding guests will remember the food, drinks, and music – not the flowers or decorations.

Let's discuss the wedding tax for both flowers and decorations. We'll start with the decorations.

Wedding Tax: Decorations

I'll give three examples of some of the mark-ups you should expect to see when it comes to decorations. However, even though I will only provide three examples, you should expect to see similar mark-ups for any decoration. I'll start with the centerpieces.

1. The centerpieces are going to be the decorations that are at the center of every table. They are typically a combination of some type of floral design, glassware, and candles. Our decorator tried to pitch us on this "floating candle" setup. This setup was a series of three wine-style glasses of varying heights filled with water.

   Inside each glass was a floating container with a candle inside of it. The candles were about half an inch thick. This setup cost $35 per table. Three glasses, with water inside of them, and a 50 cent half-inch candle was $35. PER TABLE. WHAT?!
2. Many couples decide to get a backdrop for their sweetheart table. For those of you that may not be familiar with the backdrop, it is essentially fancy linen held up by a couple of poles. Sometimes instead of linen, there is a green or floral design, typically made from plastic or paper-like material, but occasionally actual greens and flowers if the couple feels like splurging. We were quoted $900 for a white linen backdrop.
3. You may be considering obtaining a card box for your wedding. The card box is supposed to be box, chest, or storage container type thing that all of the wedding guests put their wedding cards and cash gifts into. Our florist quoted us $300 to rent their glass card box.

I was reasonably certain I could buy these materials at Ikea and recreate the floating candle setup as well as the backdrop and card box for a lot cheaper than what we were being quoted. After some quick internet browsing, it turned out that, yes, I could, in fact, recreate all of those decorations for at least one-fifth of the price.

The price of the card box, in particular, seemed a lot higher than it should have been. A quick search showed that you could purchase a

- Two corsages for mothers
- Nine boutonnieres for the groom, best man, groomsmen, father of the bride, the ring bearer (tiny flowers pinned to chest – I think these were $45 per boutonniere)
- Two white roman columns - $300
- One white runner
- Chiffon draping in aisles of the church
- Six pews decorated with flowers

My contract did not contain a specific breakout for each item above, unfortunately. This was an oversight on my part. Make sure yours does. Luckily, when we came in for our second visit to discuss decorations at the reception venue, we asked for a more detailed breakdown. Below are our pre-tax reception decoration costs:

- Mr. & Mrs. White runner for our dais (long white cloth with a Mr. & Mrs. sign that you could buy at Michaels) - $350
- Two tablecloths with some white rose petals - $60
- Three-pole backdrop - $700 (negotiated down from $900)
- Nine centerpieces @ $65 each - $585 (simple 15% flower & 85% greens in a box – NO FLOATING CANDLES)
- Two sets of fancy floating candles for our wedding table - $100

The total amount we spent on the florist after taxes was $3,907.

Our Experience

Our florist was on our venue's list of preferred vendors. We met with the florist more than a year out from our wedding. Our initial meeting was to discuss basic things such as how many groomsmen and bridesmaids there would be, how many parents or grandparents would be attending, and what type of flowers did we want for our wedding party. They also asked how many tables we expected to have to get an idea of how many centerpieces would be needed.

This was pretty much all the contact we had with them until about six weeks before our event. Then, we discussed more specific details, such as what kind of floral and non-floral decorations we wanted at our ceremony and our reception. Other details, such as the start time of the ceremony and the start time of the reception, were also discussed.

On the day of our wedding, the florist was *supposed* to set up the floral arrangements at the church and at the venue. They had the exact name and address of both the church and the venue. When I arrived at the church, I noticed that there were no flowers or decorations at all. Guests were already starting to take their seats. The ceremony was supposed to begin soon. WHERE THE HELL WERE OUR FLOWERS?!

I called my wife and asked her if our florist had called or anything because the flowers were not set up. She completely lost her shit and called the florist. While I was waiting for her to call me back, I briefly considered plundering the rose bushes of some of the houses nearby and trying to arrange them at the end of the pews.

Luckily, before I had the chance to follow through with that horrendous idea, my wife called me back. It turned out that even though we gave the florist the correct name and address of the church, they STILL managed to go to the wrong church and set up the flowers there. This was a lot for me to process. How could you go to the wrong church even though we provided the correct name and address? Was there also a wedding at the first church that the florist went to? Did the priest just think to himself, "Oh, the good Lord has graced us with beautiful flowers today? God truly works in mysterious ways"?

I told myself that if my wife got to the church before the flowers did, then I would be demanding a refund. Unfortunately, or fortunately, depending on your point of view, my wife was so late to the church, that the setup crew was actually able to wrap up the flowers from the wrong church, drive them over to the right church, and set them all up before my wife got to the church, all while our guests sat and watched, of course. Sigh. I was really hoping for some of my money back. Oh well.

Luckily, the florist didn't screw up the venue. When my wife and I arrived at the venue, we were happy with how the venue had been decorated. Everything was in the proper place, and no decorations were missing. We were especially delighted that they were able to find the correct venue on the first try, which just goes to show how low the bar was set at that point.

The wedding tax is supposed to be justified by the fact that vendors go above and beyond for your wedding to make sure that nothing goes wrong. Given that we did not have that experience, we have this advice to give:

1. Don't overspend here. Obviously, you want your wedding to look beautiful, so you may feel like you want to go all out on decorations. Well, I got some news for you. After a few months, almost nobody will remember your centerpieces. Most people will not remember what your sweetheart table looked like or what flowers the wedding party had. Do you know what they will remember? If they had fun or not or whether they were drinking and dancing all night.

    You can have a perfectly decorated wedding, but if your guests aren't having fun, then that is the memory that's going to stay with them. Even a year after our wedding, we have had some of our guests tell us how much fun they had at our wedding, but

absolutely nobody has ever brought up our wedding decorations or floral arrangements. Ever.
2. We certainly felt we were being charged much more than the materials were worth. We get that you do have to consider the labor cost of delivery and setup. However, if you have the time for it, you can save a ton of money on decorations if you make it into a DIY project.

   A coworker of mine mentioned that his brother and sister-in-law ended up doing this. They even had members of their wedding party deliver the decorations beforehand to their outdoor venue, and were able to have custom-made decorations for only the cost of the materials used to make them. Smart folk.
3. My wife and I didn't ask what types of greens or flowers were being used for our decorations and how they affected costs. In hindsight, this was a mistake. You should get this information from your florist so that you can do some research and see whether they are marking you up a ton or not.

   You can compare their quotes to other flower shops or hardware stores that sell gardening materials such as Home Depot or Lowe's. At worst, it won't impact your decision, but it could convince you that maybe you should choose a cheaper flower than the default presented to you.
4. Make sure that whatever flowers you do end up wanting will be in-season at the time of your wedding. In-season flowers tend to be cheaper than out-of-season flowers. If you bring this up to your florist, and you realize they are charging you the same amount regardless of whether the flowers are in-season or not, then this could be a sign to keep looking, or it could be an excellent negotiating opportunity for you.

- How the officiant typically goes about personalizing wedding ceremonies for their clients. This is important because you want to make sure that your ceremony feels personal and not like somebody is unenthusiastically reading the same script for the thousandth time.
- Building on the previous point, you should also discuss any ideas you have to make your ceremony more personal. You can do this by telling the officiant what you want to be included in your ceremony, such as any readings, prayers, or speeches.
- Make sure to discuss the length of your ceremony with your officiant. Most ceremonies that are performed by an officiant tend to be around 20 minutes long, 30 minutes tops. However, if you absolutely cannot wait to get married, you could technically ask the officiant to structure your ceremony like so:

Officiant: Do you?

Bride: Yes.

Officiant: Cool. Do you?

Groom: Yes.

Officiant: Sweet. I now pronounce you husband and wife.

While I'm sure the officiant would appreciate getting paid their usual fee for performing a five-second ceremony; please make sure your future spouse is agreeable to this idea.

For those of you that want a ceremony with a religious feel, but without actually jumping through the hoops that your religion may require, there are retired pastors, rabbis, and other religious figures that still officiate weddings in a religious manner without being as strict as a traditional religious wedding would require. Lastly, regardless of whether you choose an officiant or a religious authority, there are certain legal requirements that you will need to meet. I will discuss these in detail later in the book.

If you opt for the religious wedding ceremony, there are a lot more things that you need to consider. I will talk about this process in general, but then also provide detail on specific steps in the process for a Catholic wedding, since that is what my wife and I opted for.

Religious Ceremony

If you are planning to have a religious wedding ceremony, there are some things you will need in advance of this.

- You will need to have proof that you are a full-fledged member of your religion. Whether Jewish, Christian, or Muslim, your religious authority will be required to confirm that you are a fully initiated member of your faith. Unfortunately, having memorized a few prayers doesn't count as proof.
- If you are not a fully initiated member of your religion, your religious authority will most likely require you to complete the remaining steps before being able to proceed. If you are converting from a different religion, then you will most definitely be required to complete a religious education and initiation before being able to continue.

At this point in time, if your wedding is still a long way off, they should be able to put your wedding on the books regardless of whether you have religious education or initiation to fulfill. Once you have submitted all documents, you will be able to discuss what the rest of the process will be like with your religious authority. This may include:

- Taking a seminar or course specifically for couples planning on being married.
- Donating to your place of worship in exchange for performing your ceremony, often mandatory.

- Discussing what religious texts you would like read at your ceremony and any additional rituals that should be performed. For example, my wife is Filipina, and they have several wedding rituals that you don't always see performed at non-Filipino weddings.

  Which reminds me, if you have cultural-specific wedding rituals that you would like done at your wedding, try to find a religious authority that is also from this culture. They will be much more likely to be open to performing these rituals. If your religious figure is very strict, not from your culture, and is asked to perform these rituals, they may not see them as a standard practice of your religion and may refuse to perform them.

- If your religious ceremony typically involves a sermon, you should discuss with your religious authority what kind of sermon will be preached. Keep in mind that they may not even give you the option to suggest different themes for the sermon, as they are the religious authority, and you are not. However, it does not hurt to try. I will explain later when I discuss our wedding ceremony experience why you should at least give it a shot.

What to Do If your Religious Authority Makes You Uneasy

You may realize that you are not as comfortable with your religious authority as you thought you would be. Religious bodies, especially the stricter ones, tend to feel that they do not need to cater to you because they are the authority, and you are the worshipper. Technically, they are within their right to perform your ceremony how they see fit, and unlike your other vendors, you can't just demand that they do what you say.

However, just because you can't demand that they fulfill your requests, doesn't mean you are powerless. There should be nothing stopping you from seeking out a different place of worship if you feel that is the best course of action. If you meet the requirements to get married by your religion, the particular place of worship should not matter as long you find an equivalent place of worship elsewhere. You may need to register as a member of this other church, synagogue, mosque, etc. But, as long as you jump through the necessary bureaucratic hoops, there shouldn't be any issues.

Here's a brief story about why I think you should keep this option on the table. A relative of mine had actually met with a priest from a Catholic church to discuss having their wedding ceremony there. The priest, for whatever reason, disregarded my relative the entire meeting while only speaking to and making eye contact with my relative's fiancé. Additionally, the priest had condescendingly implied that they were only getting married for citizenship papers, even though they are both American citizens.

After that meeting, they decided to look for a different church. If you end up having a similarly unpleasant experience, feel free to explore a different place of worship. After all, if the religious authority treats you poorly, they have nobody to blame but themselves when you go look for another one. There will be another place of worship willing to take your mandatory donation.

The Catholic Wedding: The Unexpected Penance We Had to Endure

WARNING The material in this chapter will be equivalent to being strapped to a chair while a salesperson tries to pitch you on all of the benefits that come with buying a timeshare, and slapping you awake anytime you start to doze off. However, the "Our Experience" section at the end of this chapter will have a wedding horror story that all readers can benefit from reading, or at least have a good laugh at my expense. So if you are not Catholic, feel free to skip ahead to the "Our Experience" section at the end of this chapter. Now that you've been adequately warned let's get started.

Whether you are a devout worshiper, or only doing the Catholic wedding because your parents will never let you live it down if you don't, this section should answer any questions regarding the Catholic wedding. Here I will provide a checklist of items that you need to complete for a Catholic wedding:

1. Before doing anything else, you must be a registered member of your parish. Both of you. This requires you to go to the rectory and fill out some paperwork. This is needed for Church records when the time of the wedding comes.

    It doesn't take that much time, so do this as soon as you can. If you haven't been to church since your Confirmation, never fear. They don't keep an attendance record of all the times you've missed Mass. They're happy just to sign you up.

2. The wedding is supposed to occur at the parish of the bride. If you, as a couple, decide that you would prefer to have your wedding at the church of the groom, you must obtain a written letter from the bride's parish stating that they allow the marriage to take place at the groom's parish. If you both are registered to the same parish, then this is not necessary.

3. You will need to gather some paperwork such as a birth certificate, baptism certificate, and Confirmation certificate. If you are wondering about First Communion, proof of First Communion isn't required because it is a prerequisite to doing your Confirmation. If you were baptized in a different country like my wife and I were, you are expected to go in person or send somebody to go to the church in which you were baptized to obtain a certificate.

   I had no idea which church in Ecuador I was baptized in, and my mother did not remember either. Luckily my grandmother figured it out, so my mother was able to go in person, since she resides in Ecuador, and obtain the Baptism certificate. She ended up sending me a scanned copy, which was sufficient for the priest at my parish. Some other priests might be stricter about obtaining an original copy, but luckily mine wasn't.

   The same process applies to your Confirmation certificate. It can be a pain in the ass to track down all of this paperwork, especially if you never retained any of it, but it is all required, so you don't exactly have a choice.

4. You can now make an appointment to meet with a priest! At your appointment, once you show all of your required paperwork, you can officially get your wedding on the books. Again, the farther out you begin to plan your wedding, the more likely your church is to be available on your desired date. If you never completed your Confirmation or you are converting from another religion, you will have to undergo religious education.

   I am not entirely sure how long this takes for adults, as I did it as a child in Sunday school. However, the priest should still allow you to get your wedding date on the books with the expectation that all religious education and initiation will be done before then.

At this meeting, the priest should also give you some materials for your wedding. The packet should contain:

    a. A form where you identify which two of your wedding guests will serve as witnesses and sign your wedding certificate.

    b. Information regarding the completion of the pre-Cana seminar.

    c. A book to help you choose what readings and which rituals will be performed at the ceremony.

    d. A notice that states how much the (mandatory) donation will be for performing the ceremony. You might be reading this and thinking about trying to negotiate the donation amount. It is certainly possible to do this, but you will need to prove to the church that you are not doing too well financially. This means, if you are spending thousands of dollars on a venue, photographer, etc., then the church will likely reject your request for a smaller donation. Because, if you can afford to spend money on a "non-essential" item such as a venue, then you can afford to pay the much smaller donation to the church. Just keep that in mind.

5. The Pre-Cana. This is a required seminar/workshop for all aspiring married couples. From what I've heard, the themes of these Pre-Cana seminars can vary slightly depending on who is leading the seminar, which can be either a priest or an approved couple that has been married by the Catholic church.

The couple that led our seminar focused on marital advice in the areas of communication, conflict resolution, and how to incorporate God into our marriage. There were also some assignments on why we were getting married, what we thought were the strengths and weaknesses of our future spouse and other similar assignments.

To be honest, some of these questions seemed like they were intentionally designed to instigate an argument. It was almost as if we were on a game show designed to weed out some couples. "Contestant #1, please tell your fiancé the top three things you dislike about her and provide examples. If your relationship survives this round, you will be advancing to the bonus round, where you will be asked to explain why you would be a better parent than her".

The game show, erm, I mean, seminar, will most likely take around a total of 8 hours. You should have the option of either doing the whole 8 hours in one shot or splitting it up into smaller sessions. We opted for four two-hour sessions since it worked better with our schedule. Upon completion of the pre-Cana seminar, the leader of the workshop will give you a certificate of completion stating that your relationship survived "The Weakest Link: Wedding Edition".

You will need to turn this certificate in to your priest. So don't lose it! Lastly, you don't need to do the pre-Cana right away, but you won't be able to proceed with the rest of the process until it is completed.

6. Set a second meeting with the priest now that you have fulfilled all of your requirements. Here you will:
    a. Provide your preferences for which readings and rituals you would like performed at your wedding. You will also have the option of assigning some of your wedding party to the readings and rituals.

     b. Set a date for your wedding rehearsal if you haven't already. Confirm with the priest that they are not double-booking your slot. You will have to make your payment either at this meeting or soon after.
7. Meet with the music director to discuss which songs you want to be played during your ceremony. Unless your church is lenient, they will only play religious music. Therefore, you probably won't be able to request any Hip Hop, Rock, or other genres that the Catholic Church considers to be devil music.
8. Go to your rehearsal at the church. This will just be practice for the actual wedding ceremony. Make sure that everybody knows what they are supposed to do. If your lectors are not experienced at public reading, ensure that your lectors know how to read the passage without rushing through it. Otherwise, your wedding ceremony will end up turning into a speed reading competition.

Our Pricing

It was a $700 (mandatory) donation, with a $400 additional deposit that was to be given back to us as long as the ceremony started on time. If the service did not start on time, the church was allowed to keep the $400. If the flower girls dropped flower petals on the ground, the church was allowed to keep the $400. If Jesus himself did not make a miraculous appearance at our wedding, the church was allowed to keep the $400. Okay, now this last bit was an exaggeration, but spoiler alert: we didn't get our deposit back.

Our Experience

We did the Catholic wedding and didn't have much trouble obtaining all of the paperwork required for the ceremony. We picked a

Filipino priest from my parish since my wife wanted to make sure we got to do all of the traditional Filipino rituals for the ceremony. Honestly, everything went pretty smoothly up until the week of the wedding. We finished our pre-Cana with no issues, and our meetings with the priest went well. However, during the week of the wedding, everything fell apart.

Even though we got our wedding on the books a year in advance and confirmed our rehearsal date more than a month out, we somehow got our rehearsal slot double-booked. When we showed up to our rehearsal at the church the day before our wedding, the priest informed us that there was an event that was supposed to start just half an hour after our rehearsal was supposed to start. WHAT???

To make matters worse, a few of our wedding party showed up late, so we had maybe 20 minutes to rehearse our wedding. After five minutes, it became painfully clear to me that there was absolutely no way in hell that we were going to be prepared for this ceremony. The priest was trying to rush us through the rehearsal, but nobody knew what it was they were supposed to be doing. It was at this point that I accepted our actual wedding ceremony might be a clusterfuck.

On the day of our ceremony, my groomsmen, family, and I showed up on time. My wife and her bridesmaids were late because of our super-committed, but overzealous photographer. So bye, bye $400. Once the ceremony started, everything seemed to be going more or less okay despite the lack of practice.

However, when it came time for the members of our wedding party that we selected to read from the Bible, we realized that we didn't set up a time for them to practice public reading. They blazed right through the passage without pausing, so that we could barely understand what they were saying. It almost felt as if they were competing to see who could read the fastest.

Oh, but the real kick in the nuts occurred when the priest was delivering his homily. To give some context, one of the reasons we chose this Filipino priest in particular, was because his homilies were usually short, sweet, and uplifting. Our wedding day was the day he decided it was going to be Opposite Day.

His homily started with a bit of humor, which lasted for about five minutes. He then proceeded to spend the next 45 minutes, talking about divorce statistics and how marriage isn't taken seriously enough. I almost pulled out my phone and began googling what divorce proceedings entail since it seemed that's where my marriage was headed anyway.

After almost an hour of my wife and I sitting front and center, while our wedding guests tried not to cringe at all the divorce statistics talk, we were finally released from this cruel and unusual punishment. Honestly, I half expected him to try to refer us to a good divorce lawyer at the end of the homily, even though divorce isn't allowed in the Catholic religion. After that sermon from hell, we got through the rest of the divorce hearing, I mean, wedding ceremony, with only minor hiccups despite the lack of practice. All in all, our wedding ceremony lasted for almost two hours.

At the very end of the ceremony, we were supposed to walk out and be greeted by our wedding party, but our priest and photographer were not on the same page. So, our guests ended up awkwardly walking out on their own while the photographer was busy taking our photos. My wife was not exactly pleased with any of this, and we thought our wedding day was ruined, but thankfully our reception more than made up for the ceremony.

Given our subpar experience, we HIGHLY recommend you do the following:

1. Double-check, triple-check, quadruple-check that your rehearsal date and wedding date are not double-booked. Our wedding would have gone a bit more smoothly if we had actually had the chance to have a proper rehearsal.
2. Make sure your priest and photographer/videographer are on the same page about logistics or details.
3. For the love of God, if you are having a religious ceremony, talk to your priest, rabbi, imam, etc., about whatever sermon they plan on giving. Again, they are the religious authority, and there is no guarantee that they will be open to your suggestions about the topic or length of the sermon. However, given our experience, we highly recommend you at least give it a shot.

Are you still awake?? Feel free to give yourself a recovery day after reading through this section. I certainly gave myself a week of recovery after writing it, so I figure you at least deserve a day.

Wedding Limo & Other Transportation: All That Matters is That You Get There

One sometimes-overlooked detail is transportation. In particular:

1. How will you be getting to your ceremony and reception venue?
2. If the ceremony and the reception are not taking place at the same location, will you be providing transportation for your guests?

Transportation logistics are not exactly at the forefront of everybody's mind, but they do matter. I'll divide this section into two parts. The first part will focus on transportation for the bride and groom, and the second part will focus on transportation for the guests.

Transportation for the Bride & Groom

You have several options here. As usual, each will have its pros and cons.

- Private Limousine – The pro of hiring a private limo is that they will run on your schedule, will fit all of your bridesmaids or groomsmen, and will generally do whatever you ask of them, but the con is that they can be pricey. When we were looking at limo companies, we saw the price vary between $1,000 - $2,000 for the day, depending on how big the limousine was.

  Keep in mind that the bride and groom will most likely be coming to the wedding from different locations, and since many people in the United States believe that a groom should not see his bride until the ceremony, you may need to get two private limos.

When it comes to choosing a limo company, keep doing what we've already discussed. Read reviews on the company (especially punctuality!), meet them in person to see if you like them, and know your contract inside and out.

- Private Car – By this I mean either a relative or friend drives you where you need to go, or you drive yourself in your car. The pro is that you know the person, you still have a private vehicle, and you will pay little to nothing. The con is that you may not be able to fit all of your groomsmen or bridesmaids in one car unless you are in a minivan.

For those of you that grew up in large families with stubborn parents, you may be used to cramming everyone in the backseat or even the trunk. While this technically is a feasible way to transport your wedding party, I'm pretty sure nobody wants to simulate a kidnapping by being transported in a trunk.

- Car Rental – I don't mean go out and rent a Toyota or Honda. At that point, you would be better off taking a cab or Uber (see next section). If you're going to the trouble of renting a car, you should travel in style. Some companies have vintage car rentals for weddings. You can rent a vintage Rolls Royce from the 1950s or 1960s and make your wedding feel like something out of one of those old-timey movies.

You can even find an exotic car rental agency that rents out Ferraris or other sports cars. The pro of renting a fancy car is that you get to travel in style and feel like a boss on your wedding day. The con is obviously the money and the fact that your fancy car rental will most likely only fit two people. Around the NYC area, an exotic car rental was going to cost over $1,000 for a day.

Just imagine the roar of the engine, the screeching of the tires, the raw horsepower as you grip the steering wheel... and keep imagining this as you and your Ferrari remain idling in New York City traffic while surrounded by Prius'.
- Taxi or Public Transportation – If you do not own a car, do not have a friend or relative available to drive you and did not budget for a private limo, you can call a taxi or Uber to take you where you need to be. If you're really on a budget, the bus or train works just fine.

The con is that you will not be traveling in style and may end up being paired with a newbie Uber driver that doesn't know what they're doing, or you may be stuck riding a crowded bus or train. The pro is that you can't exactly get much cheaper than this unless you bike or walk to wherever you need to be.

Transportation for the Guests

Realistically, unless you live in a big city, I would imagine that most of your wedding guests would have come in a car, so they will probably be able to drive themselves in the event that your ceremony and reception are not at the same place. However, for all of you big city folk out there, here are some options for transporting your wedding guests from your ceremony to your reception:

- Charter Bus – In the NYC area, a 30-person bus could be rented for $350 for one hour. This is a bit small, but larger options were available for a higher price. The pro is that everybody is on the same bus and will get there at the same time with very little coordination. The con is that if you have a lot of wedding guests, you may have to rent a much larger, much pricier bus.

- Uber Events – You can create an event using Uber Events. In doing this, you can select a time range that Ubers will be available to book and the maximum number of Ubers that can be booked. You will receive a code that you will have to send to your guests. When they book their Uber, they will use your code, and the Uber will be charged to you. Once the time window closes, or the booked Ubers reach the maximum limit you set, then the event is closed out.

The pro is that once you send out the code, your wedding guests can handle their own travel, and this option will most likely be cheaper than renting a bus. The con is that there is potential for this to be an inefficient process. For example, you may have two wedding guests booking an Uber for themselves only when they could fit two or three more guests with them depending on the size of the Uber. This is why it is vital to communicate how Uber events work beforehand. I believe Lyft also has an event option so other rideshare apps may have them as well.

Our Experience

My wife stayed at a hotel the night before our wedding. She chose to have her brother-in-law drive her and the bridesmaids to the ceremony, and then from the ceremony to the reception venue.

I am a born and raised New Yorker. It seemed only logical to me that I take the subway to my wedding ceremony. Although some of my friends think I am a lunatic for doing this, I had no issue riding the subway in my wedding tux. To get from the ceremony to the reception, my new brother-in-law gave me a ride.

Since our wedding ceremony was not in the same location as our reception venue, we decided we would provide transportation for our wedding guests. We created an event using Uber Events and asked a couple of our wedding guests beforehand if they could please be in charge of the event code and efficiently group our other wedding guests that required transportation into Ubers. I also told my groomsmen about the code, assuming that they would be able to handle this on their own.

I'll admit, if your wedding guests do not have their act together, this can be a pain in the ass. My groomsmen were all going to order themselves their own Uber before I stepped in and reminded my beloved friends that each Uber could in fact fit at least four people. Although, perhaps after enduring the most depressing wedding ceremony of their life, they just couldn't wait to get out of there and begin drinking on my behalf. Anyways, each Uber cost $30 - $40 at the time, so we could not complain about the pricing.

Hey, We're Finally Done With Vendors – Just Kidding Here's Some More Advice

Now, I know I have said this a few times already, but make sure to shop around! Don't just sign on with the first vendor you meet. See what else is out there and see if there's any room for negotiation. For example:

- Vendors may offer a discount on their services if you are purchasing a lot of items from them. If this is the case for you, you should definitely inquire about a potential discount.
- If one vendor that you were not too excited about is cheaper than the vendor you actually do want, see if they will match the cheaper vendor's prices, or at least come closer to it.
- If the vendor you want isn't willing to negotiate on price, then you need to do some thinking. I know I have been very focused on price so far, but while the price is important, it's not all about the money (did I really just say that??). Ask yourself, why do you want that vendor? Is it because they are promising you the world? Or is it because they made you feel comfortable with the whole process while no other vendor could?

    At the end of the day, if the vendor has been able to gain your trust without them just saying whatever it is you wanted to hear to make you sign, then it's probably worth the extra money. If things go sideways, you want to be able to trust the vendor to handle it.

Once you've met with all of your vendors, you are going to have to make a final decision on which ones you want to sign with and which packages, in particular, you want to buy. Everybody's priorities will be different, but I will say again, the photographer and DJ are areas that I recommend investing more of your budget in. However, this doesn't mean you need to buy everything that the DJ and photographer are selling. Ask yourself questions like:

- How much value is this item actually adding to my wedding?
- Do I really need videography in addition to photography? Or is videography redundant?
- A light show sounds cool, but will it still be as cool during a daytime wedding?
- Do I need the most beautiful, most expensive bouquet? Or is a cheaper one fine given that I will only be holding it during the ceremony and then tossing it to my wedding guests?

After asking yourself questions like these and making final decisions, you are almost ready to sign. There is still one factor left to consider: payments.

Payments Schedule: Why You Should Absolutely Pay Attention to This

Payments will be the last major topic I bring up regarding vendors. There are three possible payment schedules you can set up for your vendors. They are:

1. The default payment schedule set out by the vendor. These will typically consist of a deposit (approximately $1,000 per vendor for us) and then large, infrequent payments until a month before the wedding. In the month of the wedding, you will be expected to pay the remaining balance, typically 25% - 50% of the total balance.
2. A negotiated payment schedule where you put down less of a deposit and make smaller, more frequent payments.
3. A one-time upfront payment for the full balance. If you are able to choose this option, then you probably don't need this book.

The type of payment schedule you choose will depend on your needs and financial situation. If you are not worried about paying large lump sums, the default payment schedule that the vendor will give you is probably fine. However, if you don't have stacks of cash lying around and think it may be difficult for you to gather up funds to make those payments while also paying your everyday bills, I recommend that you ask the vendors before signing about changing the payment schedule to monthly or weekly.

Some Advice on Payments

I know by now I probably sound like an old uncle that cornered you at a family gathering and is lecturing you on financial responsibility. Moreover, just like this annoying uncle, I'm going to continue giving advice you're probably tired of hearing. Namely:

1. Don't just use your credit card or take out a personal loan to pay for your venue and vendors. I understand that this is probably the biggest day of your life so far, but you don't want to start your marriage with a load of debt, especially if you already have student loans to consider. Please be financially responsible.
2. Think ahead. Having the mindset of "It's okay, just splurge now and worry about the bill later", can end up causing a cash flow crunch down the road. Other expenses that will come up that you need to consider, such as the wedding dress, tuxedo, bachelor party, etc. If you are planning on going on your honeymoon right after your wedding, you will need to book your travel while you are making vendor payments.
3. Plan for the unexpected. There are always unforeseen expenses. When you are allocating your budget for vendor payments, make sure to save some room for emergency expenses. For example, I had to replace my wife's engagement ring stone a month before the wedding because it popped out. Luckily, I had set aside some of our budget for unforeseen circumstances, so even though it hurt my soul, replacing it wasn't a problem.

For the record, my wife and I did not take on any debt to pay for our wedding. We butted heads a few times when I thought that we were going to overextend ourselves financially because she wanted to pay for a product or service that I didn't think was going to enhance our wedding. However, at the end of the day, I think we were able to control our spending so that it was manageable to us. I will discuss in the next chapter how you can approach managing finances with wedding payments coming due.

Sign Your Vendor Contracts

Now that you have decided on what you wanted, negotiated, and agreed on a payment plan, it is time to sign your contract. Read your agreement and make sure that everything you discussed is explicitly written out.

- Make sure it indicates when payments are due and how much those payments will be.
- Make sure that all of the services or products you are purchasing are clearly listed out.
- Double-check and triple-check it. The last thing you want is for you not to get everything that you paid for because it was left off the contract, and the vendor forgot about it or the person you made the agreement with no longer works for that vendor.
- Once you have quadruple checked everything, make peace with the amount, services, and payment schedules and sign.

Finally, Some Downtime. Here's How to Effectively Utilize It

After booking your venue and all of your vendors, ideally a year or more in advance, you will have a long period of downtime. By this, I mean that all of your major areas have been booked, and you won't be forced to actively plan for your wedding because there are no immediate deadlines. The next time your vendors or venue will be actively reaching out to you to schedule your final appointments will most likely be about four weeks before your wedding, possibly even six weeks before if your vendor has the availability.

Initially, my wife and I wanted to begin discussing final details and preparations 6 – 8 weeks before our wedding so that we wouldn't be so squeezed for time during the month of the wedding. We tried to schedule meetings with our vendors and venue, but with the exception of the florist, none of them wanted to meet with us that far out.

It seemed to us that our vendors and venue were so busy finalizing details and logistics of their events coming due in 2 weeks or less, that they did not have any mental capacity left to worry about final details for events coming due farther out than that. As a result, despite our asking, we were not able to schedule a meeting with any of our vendors until 3 – 4 weeks out and continued to have meetings up until 5 – 7 days out. Perhaps your experience will be different, but be prepared to be bombarded with wedding planning details a month before your wedding.

All of the above being said, that does not mean that there is nothing you can do during your extended downtime period. Below is a list of items that you should be handling during your downtime so that you save yourself stress later:

- Wedding dress

- Bridesmaids dresses & groom/groomsmen tuxes
- Wedding bands
- Honeymoon (if you plan on taking one soon after your wedding)
- Bridal Shower & bachelor/bachelorette party (if you plan on having one)
- Save-the-dates & wedding invitations
- Looking at ways to cut costs or manage finances & look for deals on other wedding-related items

I'll discuss each of these and tell you what my wife and I ended up doing, but I won't be as detailed as the vendor discussions since these expenses are chump change compared to a vendor or venue. Let's start with the wedding dress.

Wedding Dress: To Rent, Or Not To Rent, That Is the Question

The wedding dress is obviously an important part of the wedding process. It's what the bride-to-be will be wearing as they walk down the aisle and say their "I dos". However, I do not think this is an area where you should devote a ton of your budget to. The fact is that most brides wear their wedding dress only once: on their wedding day. Sure, some brides may also wear it many years later during a vow renewal or similar event, but most likely, you will need to have the dress altered unless you are in the same exact shape you were in on your wedding day.

Some couples may want to pass their dress down to their children as an heirloom so that they will use it as their dress when their special day comes. However, it is very likely that wedding dress styles will change by the time their child is set to be married and that they will want a dress more to their taste. So for a dress that will most likely be used 1 – 2 times, is it worth it to drop a ton of money? In case it hasn't been obvious, my opinion on the matter is a hard "NO".

To provide some context, the average amount spent on purchasing a wedding dress in 2018 was approximately $1,600, but if you think you want to spend $10,000 on a designer dress by Vera Wang or whoever, then as stated before, this is not the book for you.

You have a couple of options when it comes to wedding dresses. You can either buy your wedding dress or rent your wedding dress. Some of you reading this may be surprised to hear that you can rent a wedding dress – I certainly was. However, it is increasingly becoming a popular option, especially among the younger crowd. There are pros and cons to both. Let's start with buying a dress.

Buying a Wedding Dress

The upside of purchasing a dress is:

- You will be able to keep it (duh)
- Since you own the dress, the store will be able to customize the dress to your proportions for a better fit.
- Some stores, such as David's Bridal, will also give you the option to preserve your wedding dress in a compact, see-through box, which will also include a guarantee against yellowing or aging for 25 years or so.

The downside of buying your dress is:

- You will be paying more money than if you had just rented.
- Unless you choose a compact storage option like the one offered by David's Bridal, you will need to find a place to store your dress, and your dress will likely be bulky and take up a decent amount of closet space.

Renting Your Wedding Dress

If you rent a dress, some benefits you will see are:

- A lower upfront cost. Since you're only renting, you will pay much less than if you buy.
- Access to dresses that may have been previously out of your price range. One reason often given in favor of renting a dress is that fancy designer dresses become affordable.
- Not having to worry about storing a dress or preserving it.

However, renting a dress does have its downsides as well:

- Because you do not own the dress, the company that you are renting the dress from will most likely not allow any alterations

on the dress because it needs to be available for other customers once you are finished with it. Though, you may be able to request minor modifications.
- You have to be 100% comfortable and aware of the damage policy. You do not want to end up being charged full retail price because you accidentally stained the dress with wine, champagne, or the tears of the person who secretly loves you but never had the guts to tell you.

Our Experience

My wife initially was going to rent a dress due to the lower cost but ended up buying one instead from David's Bridal because she wanted a dress that would be altered to fit her form as best as possible. She ended up spending $700 for the actual dress, plus another $100 on alterations and also paid for the 25-year wedding dress preservation package. This brought the total cost of her dress to roughly $1,000, which is below average.

She was certainly happy with her wedding dress and how it fit her. However, ever since our wedding, the dress has sat in a see-through preservation box on the floor in her closet. In fact, sometimes she uses the box as a shelf for clothes she's too lazy to put away. I do not expect her to wear the dress ever again.

… Wedding Party Outfits: Your Bridesmaids and Groomsmen Should Dress to Impress, but You Should Be the Stars of the Show

The bridesmaids and groomsmen are not the stars of the show by any means. However, they still have to look nice while also making sure not to show you up. Therefore, you will have to decide what style of clothes they will be wearing. Let's start with the bridesmaids.

<u>Dresses</u>

Some brides choose to pay for their bridesmaids' dresses, while others don't. The choice is yours. I think as long as the dress you want them to buy is reasonably priced, it should be no problem for the bridesmaids to buy it. However, if the dress you want your bridesmaids to buy is a crazy expensive designer dress, then I don't think it's fair to expect them to buy it themselves. Regardless of which route you end up going, you do have to select a theme and color scheme that the dress will follow.

Folks, I assume that at least one of you knows what to do when it comes to color schemes and themes and whatnot, so I will not lecture you on what colors go best for what season or whatever because I have absolutely zero expertise when it comes to that. All I am saying is that this downtime period will be the ideal time to think about the color scheme for your wedding and how the bridesmaids' dresses will complement it.

With all that being said, just because you choose a specific theme or color, doesn't mean it will pan out in reality. For example, my wife's bridesmaids were flying in from different parts of the world. As a result, it was unrealistic to have them buy the same dress from the same store. So, my wife decided to send her bridesmaids the color scheme for the wedding and told them precisely which shade of purple they should look for.

Given that the bridesmaids had free reign to buy their dresses, the style of dresses bought were not consistent across the group. Additionally, while the colors of the dresses were very similar, they were not exactly the same. Personally, neither the difference in dress styles nor the variation in color bothered me. My wife, on the other hand, used the gigantic crayon pack from Crayola as a child that contained 50 shades of purple, and as a result, did notice that the dress colors were slightly different. Fortunately, for the safety of everybody involved, she decided the dress colors were close enough not to matter.

Tuxedos

As with the wedding dress, you have the option here to either buy or rent a tux. Gents, I highly recommend you just rent a tux. Unless you frequently go to events that require you to wear a tuxedo, there isn't that much value in buying one. Both Jos. A. Bank and Men's Wearhouse offer tuxedo rentals. I have found Men's Wearhouse to have better customer service, so that is the one I chose.

I chose a dark grey tux while my groomsmen chose light grey tuxes. My groomsmen all wore brown shoes and purple ties, while I wore brown shoes and a silver tie. My wife chose all of the colors, and not a single one of us dared to argue.

Just like with the wedding dress, my groomsmen and I did an initial fitting to get the general size of the tux, shoes, etc., and then a final fitting about two weeks before the wedding. Let me tell you, some of the shirts and pants did not at all fit on some of my groomsmen, even after measurements were taken.

However, as long as you don't skip your final fitting, it should be easy enough to switch out. Some of my groomsmen were too lazy to show up for their final fitting, so they ended up with pants that were too short or shirts that had sleeves that were too short. Some of my other groomsmen had similar problems but had them all resolved during the final fitting. Skip it at your peril.

Lastly, because my wife bought her dress at David's bridal, she was able to score some coupons for the tux rentals. We got 15% off the standard price, bringing our price to $220 each after taxes, and because I had at least six rentals in my party, I was able to get a $400 shopping spree. I recommend you look for these kinds of offers, because who doesn't like free stuff?

Wedding Bands: A Cautionary Tale

Don't forget your wedding bands! As with the wedding dress and tux, I don't think you should devote thousands of dollars to your wedding bands. Sure, you will hopefully be wearing the bands for the rest of your life, so you should make sure you like it, but no need to splurge here.

I've seen wedding bands studded with diamonds that cost almost as much as the engagement ring. Keep in mind you will be wearing this every day, and unless you remember to take it off each time you are washing dishes, sleeping, or doing other ring-unfriendly activities, there is a high chance that a stone will eventually pop out of the band. My advice, keep it simple.

When it comes to the wedding bands, you want to consider durability, appearance, weight, and definitely price. You can choose from several metals such as Platinum, Gold, Silver, Titanium, Cobalt, Tungsten, and more. There are a ton of websites that can explain the trade-offs between different types of metals much better than I can since I am not an expert on rings or metallurgy. I recommend you do your research so that you end up buying a ring that feels right.

Our Pricing

My wife and I ended up buying our bands during a holiday sale at Kay's. She chose a 10-karat white gold band studded with tiny alternating diamonds and sapphires. I chose a tungsten carbide ring with an etched design. I chose tungsten instead of gold or silver because it is supposed to be very scratch resistant. It also felt heavier than the other rings, which I liked. We bought the lifetime insurance plan for her ring and a three-year insurance plan for mine. My wife's ring cost

$825 plus $120 for insurance, while mine cost $325 for the ring and $40 for the insurance after the 25% sale discount.

Our Experience

Even though we bought our rings during a sale, we were told months later by a wholesaler jeweler appraising our rings, that we probably would have gotten better quality rings for the same price at a different jeweler. Yay for us. Additionally, after we had already paid for the rings and were just filling out the insurance information, the supervisor on duty told us that we should have waited until one month before the wedding to buy our rings so that any we could avoid any issues with our fingers potentially getting fatter or thinner and not fitting our rings. Gee, thanks for waiting until after we paid for telling us that.

Luckily, it didn't end up being a problem for us since my wife, and I didn't gain or lose too much weight from then until our wedding day. However, because of that experience with the supervisor and what the wholesaler said regarding our rings, we decided we would not be buying any more higher-priced jewelry from Kay's again.

Some Advice Regarding Jewelry Insurance

Now, I feel obligated to emphasize that you should most definitely buy insurance for your rings if you end up purchasing a band that has a diamond or other gemstone in it. In fact, any piece of jewelry should be insured if it has an expensive stone, but you must make sure you are well-versed in how your insurance policy functions. I will give two examples of why you should do this.

1. One month before our wedding, the stone popped out of my wife's engagement ring. My wife freaked out, but I was calm because I knew I had the ring insured just in case something like this happened. I go to dig up the insurance information, only to realize I never formally completed the process.

   Well, I'm sure you can imagine all of the wonderful things my wife had to say to me once it became clear that the ring was not insured, as I thought it was. I ended up buying a new stone out-of-pocket so that my wife was not wearing an empty ring on our wedding day. It was an expensive lesson in careless forgetfulness. Do not repeat my mistake.
2. When we bought the wedding band, we made 100% sure that it was insured. Eight months after our wedding, one of the sapphires popped out of my wife's wedding band. Now this time, I knew we had insurance. So, sure enough, I call up Kay's and tell them what happened so that I can get the stone replaced free-of-charge.

   Unfortunately, there was a stipulation in our insurance policy that was not made clear to us at the time of purchase. We were required to bring the ring in to Kay's twice per year for a cleaning. If we missed even one cleaning, the insurance is voided. Since we missed a cleaning already, they informed us that we would have to pay out-of-pocket to replace the stone.

   They were quoting us $425 to replace the stone... which was half the cost of the ring. To be clear, this ring had five small sapphires and four small diamonds (all low quality as we later found out) embedded into the ring. How could 1 of 9 stones cost half the value of the ring?? This brings me to my next point. If you are buying insurance, know your insurance policy inside and out.

I will close this section out by saying that we got the sapphire replaced for a much better price using an independent wholesale jeweler whom my wife and I were referred to. The jeweler also cleaned the ring and provided an appraisal, which is how we found out that even with the 25% discount, we were overcharged for the ring. Regardless, we had a much better ring buying experience with this jeweler.

Honeymoon: Start Planning Sooner Rather Than Later

If you are planning on going on a honeymoon, you should start planning during your downtime because you most certainly will not have much time to plan once your wedding planning reaches its final stages. Whether you are planning on staying at a resort or are going more for the DIY travel experience, you should, at the very least, be looking at flights and lodgings, whether they be hotels, hostels, Airbnbs, or whatever your thing is.

A "How to Plan Your Honeymoon" guide is outside the scope of this book, and could honestly be a standalone book on its own. As such, I will only give a few essential tips on honeymoon planning. They are:

- Utilize tools on the internet to help you make sure you are booking your travel at a good time. For example, if you track a flight on Google Flights, it will let you know if the prices you see for a flight are lower than usual. You can also use apps like Hopper to track flight prices and use its prediction feature, which recommends whether you should wait to buy, due to an anticipated price drop, or if you should buy now because that is as good as the price is going to get.
- Try to build a mock itinerary before booking your travel. You should google things to do, read travel blogs, or look through TripAdvisor to get an idea of what activities you can do at whichever destinations you are considering. This will also give you an idea of how long you should stay at any one place, which will, in turn, help you decide what date range you should book your travel and lodgings for.
- If you are planning to go the all-expenses-paid resort route, start looking early. Starting early will allow you to hunt for the best deals or to wait for holiday sales to occur.

The main point here, however, is that you should utilize your downtime to plan a great honeymoon instead of trying to rush it at the end. Beginning to pay off honeymoon expenses in advance, or spacing them out so that they don't all hit you at once, is also something to consider. Unless you agreed upon evenly spaced-out vendor payments, there will be a significant amount due right before your wedding. It would probably be helpful if your honeymoon expenses were not added on top of that.

Bachelor/Bachelorette Party: Enjoy Your Party, But Don't Bite Off More Than You Can Chew

You may not need to worry about expenses or planning too much when it comes to your bachelor/bachelorette party. It depends on how generous your wedding party is feeling and how good of a planner your Maid of Honor or Best Man is. However, if you think you will probably be contributing something to your party, then it's best to set some funds aside in advance for this. This is especially true if you are planning on a "destination" bachelor/bachelorette party where you fly out to Vegas or some other den of debauchery.

Even if you are planning on staying local, never underestimate how much cash you might end up dropping once you've had too many drinks, and a stripper is making them cheeks clap on your face or even doing the elephant trunk whirl. My groomsmen and I were shopping around to see how much it would cost to have a reserved table by the stage.

The owner of a strip club we requested a quote for said that the people who book tables by the stage usually end up dropping $3,000 - $5,000 in a single night, and unless we were willing to commit to spending a similar amount, he couldn't reserve the table for us. This was far out of my budget, so my best man ended up picking a different option. The point I'm trying to make is that these parties can still rack up quite the bill, so make sure you include this into your budgeting.

That being said, even if you don't plan to recreate "The Hangover" and instead prefer a classier bachelor or bachelorette party, fancy wine and cheese nights still aren't cheap. Whether you are handing a wad of singles to a dancer or swiping your card at the fanciest restaurant in town, the bill comes due.

As a final note here, I know I only talked about bachelor/bachelorette parties, but the same things should apply to a bridal shower, presumably, with less debauchery. For example, my wife wanted to do the whole "elephant trunk twirl" bachelorette party, but because she had family attending, she decided just to have a classier bridal shower at a vineyard instead. Luckily, my wife knows how to bargain, so she got a nice group discount for the event.

Save-the-Dates & Wedding Invitations: The When and Where is Important – The Paper It's Printed On, Less So

Assuming you followed the steps mentioned in the section about building your wedding list, you now have to send out a formal communication. Let's talk about save-the-dates first.

Save-The-Dates

You can create your save-the-dates using a photo service like Shutterfly, or even Walgreens' photo service. In either case, the price of your save-the-dates will vary depending on:

- The type of paper the save-the-date will be printed on
- The design choice selected
- The size of the card

I think it's fine to keep your save-the-date simple, no need to get super fancy with it. My wife and I ended up having a friend take our photo while we were in formal wear, and had it printed on a card using Walgreens' photo service. We put the date of our wedding and the city in which it would take place. We had it printed on the cheaper, more flexible card stock and paid $72 after taxes for 100 copies.

Wedding Invitations

For the wedding invitations, you'll probably want to stick with a service that has more customizable options for the invite. Technically you can still go the Walgreens route, but I think since it's the actual wedding invite, you can justify a more substantial spend on it. Assuming you will be using a more specialized service, you will be able to customize the following:

- Template design
- Font color
- Background color
- Position of text areas
- The shape of the card
- The gloss of the card
- One card vs. multi-card invitation that contains the wedding information, a meal selection card, RSVP cards, and a return envelope
- Customized laser-cut designs

We ended up using Shutterfly for our wedding invitations and chose a purple and gold single-card design cut into a bubble shape. In the age of modern technology, we didn't think the multi-card approach was necessary. We just told our invitees to text us their response. We expected most, if not all, to have no issue with attending since we had several follow-ups to confirm that the date would not be a problem. So the one-card invitation ended up suiting our needs just fine.

We also chose not to opt for a laser-cut design even though they looked impressive because they cost at least double what a standard invitation cost through Shutterfly. Fortunately, because my wife went to David's Bridal for her dress, she was able to get some coupons for wedding invitations through Shutterfly. We paid $150 for 70 invites on the fancier, stiffer card stock.

Now, I know I just spent this chapter telling you about all the different opportunities you will have for customization of your save-the-date and wedding invitation. However, if, for whatever reason, the only card printing options available to you are going to rack up a bill much larger than what I have mentioned, do not at all feel pressured to stick with the fancy design. What matters is that the guests know when and where your wedding is.

The intricate design options are just fluff. Technically, an index card with the relevant information would suffice, although my wife might have written me a note on an index card calling off our wedding had I done this. If paper invites are out of your budget, and you don't want to go the admittedly awkward index card route, then you may want to consider a paperless option such as an online invitation. These are typically free or very low cost. Since we did not go this route, I cannot give you any detailed information, so you should utilize Google for this.

When to Send Out Your Save-The-Dates & Invitations

I recommend you send out your save-the-date at least six months in advance and final wedding invitations 2-3 months in advance. This should give guests that were not on the Must-Haves list plenty of time to prepare for your wedding. Additionally, if you followed the steps in the wedding list section, there should be no surprises regarding the wedding date among your Must-Haves.

Deal Hunting & Cost Cutting: Save Now, Reap the Benefits Later

Since you will not be under any time pressure during your downtime period, you should use this as an opportunity to hunt for discounts on any remaining wedding items, as well as look to see where you can make some temporary lifestyle changes to cut costs. Let's talk deal-hunting first.

Deal Hunting

I mentioned in some of the sections previously that my wife had gotten some coupons from David's Bridal. Whether the coupons end up being from David's Bridal, or some other store, early in your downtime would be the ideal time to find these deals. We weren't expecting to find coupons for tuxes and wedding invitations at David's Bridal but did not at all complain when we did. Wedding expos or fairs may be another avenue you might want to explore to find some discounts.

If you don't find coupons for your remaining wedding needs, you can still wait for some type of holiday sale to occur. That is what my wife and I did for our wedding bands. We ended up buying our bands at Kay's after purposely waiting for President's Day Weekend and received a 25% discount off retail price. Although, as I mentioned in the wedding bands section, even when you think you're getting a great deal, you may still be getting ripped off. I guess if I wanted to be optimistic, I could say I was ripped off by 25% less than I would have been had I not waited for a sale.

Cost Cutting

Something else you should be going over during this time is what lifestyle changes you can make during this time to help you save more. For example, my wife and I reviewed all of our regularly occurring expenses, as well as our occasional expenses. We separated the necessary costs, such as bills, from recreational costs, such as eating out and did some math. We cut out almost all of our recreational spending so that we could save more for our wedding expenses and honeymoon. Some things you may want to cut out of your spending during your downtime period are:

- Eating Out/Ordering Out
- Happy Hours – Going out to bars to hang out
- Shopping – non-essential clothes, furniture, electronics, etc.
- Vacations – we needed to save all of our money and vacation days from work for the honeymoon
- Other recreational activities – movies, shows, and anything else that brings you joy

Now, we did go a bit on the extreme side when it came to saving. This doesn't mean you need to do so. The point is to look at your spending and see where it makes sense to cut back. The amount you cut back by should be determined by how many wedding expenses you still have coming due and how much non-debt capital you will have to pay for it.

My wife and I knew we would be taking a three-week-long honeymoon to Asia the day after our wedding. We also knew most of our wedding payments would come due the month of our wedding. Therefore, the logical course of action was to save extra funds early on, so that after all of our final payments were made, we would still have honeymoon money left. Keep in mind we were approaching this with the mindset that we didn't want to take on any credit card debt or personal loans.

A Breakdown of All the Small Details You Need to Finalize & How Not To Lose Your Mind

So now, it's four to six weeks until your wedding. Around this time, all of your vendors should be contacting you to set up your final appointments. I will refer to this period as crunch time since you will be bombarded with wedding planning or wedding-related items from now until your wedding is over. I will go through what you need to finalize for your venue, each of your vendors, and other wedding-related activities.

I'm not going to lie; crunch time is going to suck. You will have to balance finalizing all of the small details while also balancing work and your personal life. However, by reading this chapter, you should at least know what to expect and what to focus on. Let's start with the venue.

Venue: Select From the Defaults, Save Time & Money

Approximately three weeks before our wedding date, we were finally able to set up an appointment with our venue to discuss what our venue referred to as "finals". We met with the coordinator in charge of finals and discussed the following:

- Linen colors – napkins and tablecloths
- Seating arrangements – typically 10, 12, or 14 per table
    - As far as which guests will be seated together; you should probably start thinking about this once you know what seating arrangements your venue accommodates. Make sure to ask if infants count as a seat, or if they are fine in a stroller without taking up seating space.
    - Otherwise, common sense should be enough to get you through the seating arrangement process. Seat friends together and seat enemies apart, which is the opposite of what the colonial powers in Africa did.
    - You will most likely have some friends that don't perfectly fit into any one table. You have the option of either grouping all of your misfits into one table, or if you don't have enough misfits for one table, splitting them into several tables to fill any remaining gaps.
    - You will also probably want to have your closest family and friends seated at the tables that are closest to your sweetheart table.
- DJ setup – where the DJ & equipment is going to be situated
- Sweetheart table location and backdrop
- Wedding cake flavors and appearance
    - This required us to visit the bakery that our venue used and tasting the different options of cake, frosting, and filling while also looking at sample cake designs.
- Final payment – about a week before the wedding

- This required us to list out how many adults, children, and infants would be in attendance, as they were all different rates in our contract. Payment was required in either cash or check. In our case, the remaining balance was 50% of the total.
- Before you go to the meeting and give the final payment, you should contact your guests one last time via text or phone and confirm that they are still able to attend. Sometimes things come up with short notice, and guests can no longer make it, or there will be uncertainty as to whether they can make it.

  Sometimes people break up, and will no longer be bringing a plus-one. Seven of our guests broke up with their significant others and didn't need plus-ones anymore. That was almost $700 we saved just by asking them. Better to just check before you pay so that you can reduce your headcount.

- Other additional items that required setup:
  - An example of this is a customized seating chart. My wife created a DIY seating chart out of a window frame, some rope, super glue, and paper because she did not like the default table cards that the venue would have provided to let guests know where to sit.

    This custom seating chart was very inexpensive to make, so I couldn't complain, but it did require us to drop it off at the venue two days beforehand and let them know about the setup.
  - Engagement shot set up on an easel. Same as the seating chart, this had to be dropped off in advance.

- o   Card box for any wedding guests that would be giving cash gifts or wedding cards.

Even though I summarized this into a few bullet points, this required three separate meetings, one of which was five days before the wedding. My advice here: make any linen, silverware, & cake decisions using the default options that the venue has available. I'll give three examples of why I think you should do this:

- My wife was being picky with her colors and wanted a particular shade of purple for our tablecloths, which the venue didn't have. This would have required us to either buy those table clothes ourselves or pay additional money to the venue so that they could handle it. They're just tablecloths at the end of the day, which aren't at all the focus of the wedding. Don't waste your money here.
- The situation with the wedding cake was the same. If we wanted options that were not part of the defaults presented to us, we would have had to pay extra.
- The fussier you want to be with napkin colors or custom setups, the more meetings this will require. You will not have a ton of free time during crunch time. Spend your time and money wisely, folks.

I have found that it's the tiny details such as napkin colors, which can sometimes result in an argument. This will be a stressful time for both of you, and it will be easy to get caught up in trivial things. However, this is also the time where you need to be the most patient with each other.

After all, it would sound pretty lame if you told people the wedding was called off due to "irreconcilable differences" when it came to napkin colors. Although, I'm sure the priest from my wedding would congratulate you on splitting up before the wedding and saving him the trouble of telling you to get a divorce.

Photographer: Just Tell Them Where to Show Up

Our final meeting with the studio occurred three weeks before the wedding. We discussed mainly logistics, such as:

- Address of where the photographer was going to meet the bride
- The time that the photographer was going to meet the bride
- Address of where the ceremony was taking place
- Time the photographer and the bride should arrive at the church for the ceremony
- Expected length of the ceremony
- If we were doing a wedding procession and greeting line at the end
- Address of the reception venue
- The time that the reception was expected to start

This was one of the simpler meetings we had, as we just had to convey information that we already set up far in advance. However, I mentioned previously in this book that if you booked a photographer through a studio, you should try to meet with them before your wedding. Since this is the final phase of planning, you should ask to see if the studio knows who they are going to assign to you so that you can meet with them.

My wife and I neglected to do this, and although we were generally satisfied with our photographer, we would definitely ask to meet with our potential photographer during this time if we had to go back and do it all over again. Of course, there is no guarantee that the studio will be able to accommodate this or even know who they will assign as your photographer.

However, it's better to try to put a face to a name, so you reduce the chance of letting some random person who isn't your photographer take a whole bunch of pictures of you for their personal collection.

DJ: Choose Your Tunes, but Keep Your Audience in Mind

During our final visit to the studio, we also had a separate meeting with our DJ. We had been given a music sheet to fill out beforehand, which we then discussed with the DJ. This sheet included questions such as:

- What type of music we wanted to be played
    - Even though this was our wedding, we kept the demographic of our wedding guests in mind. For example, even if we were hardcore death metal fans (which we're not), we would not have requested any of that music since our wedding guests would probably have run to the beautiful floor-to-ceiling windows and jumped out of them.
- Any special song requests to be played
- Which songs to play for father/daughter dance & mother/son dance
- What song to play for the first dance
- Number of groomsmen, bridesmaids, & parents in the wedding party
    - They needed to know this so that they could set up the order of introductions during the reception
- Which members of the wedding party were going to make toasts
    - They needed to know this so that the MC could announce it and hand the appropriate people the microphone

My wife and I wanted to get a play-by-play of what was going to happen when. For example, we wanted to know:

- When were they planning to make the toasts?
- When were they going to start the first dance?

- How would we know it was time to take center stage on the dance floor?

You get the point. I mentioned previously that when we asked these questions, our DJ told us to relax, not to worry about it, and that they would take care of everything. My wife and I were not pleased with this response. We were nervous that something would go wrong or that our wedding would look like a mess.

However, true to his word, our DJ and his team really did take care of everything with no hiccups. Their team came and got us whenever it was time for something, and everything happened according to their plan, even though we had no idea what their plan was.

I've repeated this for a reason. I 100% understand if the wedding couple wants to know the game plan. We certainly did. However, I did appreciate that my wife and I did not have to worry about the order of events and were able to enjoy our wedding day a little bit more because of it.

My advice here is that if you trust your vendor and think they are high caliber, then it's okay to let them handle the details so that you don't stress yourself out. If you are unsure about the quality of the vendor or don't trust them all that much for whatever reason, then I would probably push to stay in the know.

Florist/Decorator: The Flor(ist) is Lava! Don't Burn All of Your Cash on Flowers

We met with our florist again approximately six weeks before our wedding to discuss what sort of designs we wanted for the centerpieces and other similar decorations. During our final meeting with the florist, approximately three weeks before our wedding, we discussed logistics and made our final payment. The exact details discussed between these two meetings were:

- Start time and address of the ceremony so that the florist's employees could set up the decorations at the wrong church
- Start time and address of the reception so that the decorations could be set up beforehand
- Additional flowers or decorations
    - This was when we finalized the centerpiece design and bridal bouquet. I have to emphasize again here; I do not recommend spending a ton of money on the bridal bouquet. There is a high chance that the wedding bouquet may start to come apart depending on how gently it is handled, especially if it's just going to get thrown. No need to spend a ton of money on something with that short of a life span.
    - Flowers for the bridesmaids and groomsmen were selected at this time
    - Floral decorations at the ceremony and reception venues were also chosen at this time
    - Extras such as the backdrop were pitched to us at this point. The florist tried to pitch us a card box as well, but for $300, no thank you. We went to Michael's and bought a card box for $25.
- There were some additional logistical issues to discuss. We wanted a set of columns that the decorators were bringing to the

church, to also be present at the wedding on either side of the sweetheart table. We were told that since this would require the employees to return to the church and transport them 3 miles to the reception venue, it would cost $350 to do it. Sigh.

To be honest, at this point, I was so fed up with the florist that I was ready to commit to carrying the columns onto the subway and taking them myself. Luckily, one of my wife's friends owned a pickup truck, and he was able to transport it and set it up for us.

Gentlefolk, do not be afraid to say "no" when your vendors are trying to upsell you on something that you are not comfortable buying. We obviously did not appreciate the amount of money the florist was attempting to charge us for seemingly basic things, so we said just flat out said "no" to some things or tried to do it ourselves.

Floral arrangements or major decorations were a little out of our wheelhouse, unfortunately, but basic things like a seating chart or card box were straightforward to make and only required us to drop it off in advance. If you're like me and end up producing a crime against humanity any time you attempt to do something artistic, get a friend or one of the members of your wedding party to help you out.

Catholic Church: Thou Shall... Confirm Logistics with the Priest

Our final meetings with the church involved finalizing which readings and rituals we wanted as well as a meeting with the music director. Specifically, we discussed:

- The scriptures we wanted to be read, as well as which members of our wedding party would be reading them
- The Filipino-specific rituals we wanted to be performed, when they would occur, and which members of our wedding party, if any, would be involved
- Which items we needed to bring as part of the rituals
   - In our case, this included a Bible, coins, veil, cord, floral offering, and fruit offering
- Which songs we wanted to be played for each part of the Mass that involved music
- Confirming a rehearsal date
- Confirming who our witnesses were going to be
   - For those that are not aware, during the Catholic wedding ceremony, there is this awkward moment towards the end where the witnesses come up to the altar to sign your wedding certificate. So make sure whomever you choose to be your witnesses is aware and comfortable with this.
- Priest-mandated divorce papers... just kidding, hahaha... *sobs*

That all seemed simple enough. However, I mentioned previously what a mess the rehearsal and ceremony ended up being. I said it before, but I will say it again:

- Double-, triple-, quadruple-, and quintuple-check that the church has no events or appointments that conflict with your

rehearsal. You want to make sure you have ample time to practice for the ceremony.
- Make sure your lectors know to slow it down when reading.
- Make sure your wedding party knows what order to march in, where to sit or stand, and where to exit.
- Practice, practice, practice, if only to avoid major screw-ups. If the screw-up is minor, chances are your wedding guests won't notice, but this doesn't mean you won't notice and get extremely pissed off.

Wedding Programs: The Perfect Way to Engage Your Guests... For All of Two Minutes

Some of you may be wondering about wedding programs. For those of you that don't know, wedding programs contain some basic information about the ceremony and the wedding party. Namely:

- The names of the bride and groom
- The names of the bridesmaids, groomsmen, and parents
- The order of events of the ceremony
- Explanations regarding any religious rituals for those that may be of a different faith
- Directions from the ceremony venue to the reception venue if they are not at the same place

Let me tell you something about wedding programs. My wife wanted programs to be made for our wedding ceremony. She took the time to make a wedding program in Microsoft Word that listed out the entire wedding party, all of the readings, songs, and rituals. She made it in a fancy looking font and created a border for the pages as well.

My wife forced me to volunteer to print out 100 copies of this split-page layout front and back, which took a while to figure out how to print correctly. I ended up having to use the printer at work to print out all those copies, effectively killing a small tree.

Then, I spent the night before the wedding stapling these all together, except I ran out of staples, and the staples that I took home from work were the wrong size. After staring dumbly at my incorrectly sized staples for five minutes, I just ended up folding the rest of the programs and hoped they wouldn't come apart when our guests opened them.

Luckily, I would say our wedding guests spent 30 seconds at most looking at the program before setting them aside. Most of my wife's wedding guests were Catholic, so they knew what was going on and didn't need the programs. Most of my guests were not religious at all and didn't care to read through the rituals or readings, so they didn't need the program either. Basically, the programs were mostly useless.

My advice: don't spend a lot of time making these programs and certainly don't spend a lot of money on them. If you really want a program, a one- or two-pager is more than enough.

Rehearsal Dinner: If You Wait Too Long to Make a Reservation, Your Only Option May End up Being the McDonald's Drive-Thru

For those of you that are like how I was and don't know a thing about weddings, the rehearsal dinner is literally the dinner after the wedding rehearsal. It is an opportunity for the parents, close family, and other members of the wedding party from both sides to interact and bond over dinner.

Now, just because this is supposed to be a dinner doesn't mean it won't stress you out. There are a few things you should consider as you set up the rehearsal dinner:

1. How many people will be coming to the rehearsal dinner? This may affect the options available to you because a large group reservation may limit you to large restaurants only.
2. Logistics, such as parking and travel time. If you are having your rehearsal dinner in a busy part of town, you may want to let your guests know where the parking garages are and which streets to avoid.
3. Who is paying for the rehearsal dinner? If your parents or soon to be in-laws want to cover the bill, then that is great. However, if, for whatever reason, the bill falls on you, then you will want to make sure you have enough set aside to cover this. For this reason, I recommend you choose a reasonably priced location – especially if you live in a more urban area, there should be plenty of quality restaurants with reasonable prices. You are already going to have a fancy dinner at your wedding. There is nothing wrong with keeping the rehearsal dinner a bit more casual.

I recommend looking for a restaurant as soon as you enter crunch time. If you wait too long to book a restaurant, you may find that some of the restaurants you were considering have already accepted other group reservations and cannot accommodate you. Reserving a restaurant further in advance also allows you to negotiate a potential group discount. In my opinion, there is no benefit to waiting for the last minute to reserve your rehearsal dinner venue, so handle this right away.

Our Experience

My wife and I were so busy with our wedding planning we completely forgot about our rehearsal dinner until about two weeks before the wedding. After doing a headcount, we realized we had approximately 35 guests that would attend our rehearsal dinner, due to how many of my wife's relatives and friends flew in from the Philippines.

This quickly ruled out our favorite restaurants as potential options, since none of them could accommodate a group this large. Some other restaurants had already accepted other large group reservations. I was about to throw in the towel and just put in a large order at Taco Bell, which, to be honest, wouldn't have been a total loss, in my opinion.

Luckily, before I put in the order for 10,000 chalupas, one of my groomsmen helped us find a large restaurant that could accommodate us and would give us a 10% group discount. It was located in a busy part of town, so we (and by we, I mean I), had to guide everybody to the most easily accessible parking garage since I did not think to look this up and communicate it beforehand.

Since the restaurant was reasonably priced, many of our guests graciously offered to pay their plates, which we are eternally grateful for. Based on our experiences, I would like to reiterate that you should start looking for a restaurant 4 – 6 weeks before the wedding, have a solid grasp of your headcount, communicate to your guests any logistical information that will help them, and know how the bill is going to be covered.

Legal Requirements

The legal requirements to get married can vary by state, but in general, you will need to obtain a marriage license. To obtain a marriage license, you will have to go to your local city or county clerk. You are generally required to provide:

1. Wedding License application & fee – fee can range from $20 - $40
2. Proper Identification – a passport or driver's license should suffice
3. Proof of Age – again, your passport or driver's license should suffice, but if not, you can always provide a birth certificate
4. Social Security Number
5. If previously married, proof that marriages are annulled, or divorce took place, or spouse is deceased

Please take note that wedding licenses do have an expiration date. They vary by state. For example, once you obtain a wedding license in New York City, you have 60 days to get married before the license expires. However, in Nebraska, you have one year to get married until your wedding license expires. I guess Nebraska wants to give you plenty of time to think your decision over, whereas New York City just wants to take your money and send you on your way.

The other legal requirement you will need is one or two witnesses to sign your wedding certificate on the day of your actual ceremony. New York City only requires one witness, but other states, such as Nebraska, require two witnesses.

Your religious authority may require a different number than your city clerk. For example, our church required us to provide two witnesses, even though New York City only requires one. Make sure you select your witnesses before your ceremony, so you don't have to ask for volunteers when the time comes.

Some Minor Things to Remember

They say the devil is in the details. While some of the smaller details can seem insignificant, they can be a real pain in the ass to deal with if you forget about them. Kind of like those times when your mother asked you to take the meat out of the freezer, and you forgot. It didn't seem like such a big deal at first until she started chasing you around the house with her sandal of choice in hand. That being said, some of the devilish details you shouldn't forget about are:

Final Fittings for Wedding Dress & Tuxes

The only thing I have to say about this is that you will do your final fittings a week or so before the wedding. DO NOT SKIP THIS. My wife picked up her dress a week before the wedding, while my groomsmen and I picked up our tuxes two days before the wedding. I will say it again, my groomsmen who skipped their final fitting, all had sizing issues that would have been quickly resolved had they just showed up. Skip at your peril.

Where to Stay the Night Before & Guest Accommodations

This is an easy one to overlook, but given the rule that the groom shouldn't see his wife until the wedding ceremony, it should be discussed who is staying where the night before the wedding. My wife wanted to spend the night with her bridesmaids, and since the majority of them flew in from out of the country, they all decided to get hotel rooms.

In fact, since several of her wedding guests were coming from New Jersey, they wanted to stay in a hotel room as well. My wife, being the problem solver that she is, ended up requesting a bunch of rooms at the same hotel and scored a group rate that gave roughly 10% -

15% off. If your guests all make their own accommodations, great. If not, this might be an excellent way to save everybody some money and have them all stay at the same location as well, which would help with them showing up on time.

I had it easy. Since my wife stayed at a hotel, I was just able to stay at home alone and stay up all night, stapling together wedding programs.

Bachelor Party/Bachelorette Party/Bridal Shower

Don't forget about your pre-wedding parties. Honestly, there isn't much planning to worry about here, assuming your best man or maid of honor handled the planning. This would be a good time to unwind from all of that stressful wedding planning. Have fun and let loose, but not so loose that you spend your month's rent or mortgage payment making it rain. Try to avoid any Las Vegas-style elopements with some of the fine upstanding individuals you meet at strip clubs.

Lastly, for all of the party animals, I would highly recommend you have your bachelor/bachelorette party a week or so before your wedding. No need for a two-day hangover to obliterate all of your brain function on the day of your wedding.

Transportation

If you are hiring a private limo, you will need to meet them in person or call them to give them the details of when to pick you up, drop you off, etc. Even if you are not hiring a private limo and a friend is giving you a ride, make sure they know all of the details so that you aren't late to your wedding. Have a backup plan just in case your driver no-shows or gets a flat tire or something. The point here is, do not forget to consider how you will be getting to your ceremony and reception venues.

If you have set up transportation for your guests, make sure to send out a communication to them about how the transportation will work. Since my wife and I did the Uber Events option, we sent the event code to a couple of people we trusted to herd the rest of our guests into Ubers efficiently.

Your Special Day Is Here... Some Advice

Your special day is finally here! All of the stressful planning is finally over, and now you get to move on to the incredible stress of surviving through your wedding! Just kidding... sort of. How about you just listen to me give some more advice?

<u>Try Not To Stress</u>

Easier said than done, I know. But, at this point, things are going to happen the way they happen. Even if you planned everything correctly, unexpected things could come up. Just because you made plans and backup plans in case something goes wrong, doesn't mean that things that are totally out of your control won't come up and ruin all of your planning. Even if a bunch of stuff does go wrong, the best thing you can do is keep a Zen attitude about it. Here's an example from our wedding to illustrate why you should do this.

My wife was so wound up on our wedding day that every little minor hiccup she noticed pissed her off. This was especially true for the wedding ceremony. I also noticed every little hiccup. However, at this point, I was painfully aware that there was nothing I could do about it. I am not a time-lord. I can't just reverse back a few minutes and try to make the mistake not happen. The best you can do is have a positive attitude about it.

For example, when I noticed that the flowers had not been set up at the church and called my wife to tell her about it, she flipped out. I don't blame her; I was damn near close to flipping out myself, especially since I already felt like the florist was trying to rip us off at every turn. When the florist's team came five minutes before my wife arrived at the church and set up the flowers with the guests already seated in the pews, I couldn't help but think that it just made us look incredibly disorganized. I know my wife felt the same way.

She let that, and all the subsequent hiccups at the ceremony pile on and totally ruin her mood. Again, I 100% do not blame her for feeling this way. I was feeling this way myself until I mentally gave myself a little pep talk. Yeah, shit happened, but it was out of my control, and I sure as hell was not going to let these screw-ups define or ruin our wedding day. I was here to marry the love of my life, and I'd be damned if I let annoying little screw-ups ruin that for me.

The funny part was that my wife and I noticed all of the errors because we knew how it was meant to be done. However, after talking to our guests, later on, most of our guests did not notice or barely noticed the majority of hiccups that occurred. Except for the flowers. Everybody noticed the flowers. At the end of the day, though, who cares about the flowers, this day is about you and your spouse. This brings me to my next point.

This Day is About You and Your Spouse

No matter what goes wrong on your wedding day, no matter which wedding guests decide to start drama or be rude, no matter what blood feuds your new in-laws may bring up, this day is about you and your spouse. Focus on that. You just got married or are getting married. This is the person you plan on spending the rest of your life with. Nothing else should really matter.

There's going to be other stressful times and fights. Marriage can be tough. A stressful wedding full of mistakes will be only the first thing in your path. Approach this problem the same way you should approach any future problem: by getting through it together.

Remember To Eat

This is an especially difficult one to remember, as odd as that may sound. Your wedding may run late, and you may miss your cocktail hour due to the photographer wanting to snap as many photos as he can of the married couple. We had a two-hour gap between the planned ceremony end time and the reception start time. However, since everything ran late and the priest gave a 45-minute sermon, our picture-taking session ended up running late as well.

We didn't get to our cocktail hour until it was already halfway done. I was starving, and I am known to fly into a furious rage when I have been deprived of precious food for too long. I know my wife was starving as well, and she doesn't take food deprivation so well either. She went into her bridal suite to de-stress. I went straight to the food trays and started piling food onto my plate.

I've read in many blogs, and also personally experienced it myself, that the wedding day is so busy that it is highly probable you won't have time to eat. I was not about to let that happen to me, especially since I did not want to assault any of my wedding guests due to my empty stomach. Luckily, the maid of honor was able to bring my wife some food, so her inner beast was quelled as well.

For the rest of the reception, our time was either spent on the dance floor, talking to guests, or taking pictures with the photographer. The only time we had an opportunity to eat again was when the sit-down meal was served. Even then, our photographer was trying to get us to take more photos, or our wedding guests would come to make conversation. You are the center of attention at this wedding, so everybody is going to want a piece of you, which brings us to the next bit of advice.

You Are Going To Be the Center of Attention: Distribute Your Time

As I said, you are going to be the center of attention. Everybody is going to want a piece of you. The photographer, your guests, the DJ or MC, your parents, etc. Don't feel obligated to spend all of your time talking to one person who refuses to let the conversation end. Make sure you, at the very least, greet all of your guests. If they are not able to have a full-blown conversation with you, they know it's because you are being pulled in eight different directions at once.

At least any human being with average emotional intelligence should know that. For the ones who don't, make sure to politely excuse yourself. To be fair, your photographer will probably drag you away before anyone person tries to trap you into a 30-minute conversation anyway. Our photographer certainly prevented any of our conversations from lasting more than a couple of minutes since he was always coming back to make sure we could take more photos.

Thank Your Guests

At some point towards the end of your reception, the MC should come up to you and your spouse so that you can make an announcement in which you thank your guests for coming and give a small speech about your wedding or whatever else you'd like. You should think about what you want to say in advance. There's no need to prepare a 10-minute long speech, but you should have some general ideas so that you don't get handed the mic and start to go "uhhhhhh, yea, ummm, thank you all for coming, umm, have a great day".

Don't Forget Tips for Your Vendors

Ah, tipping. Everybody's favorite thing in the world. This is technically supposed to be entirely up to you. However, our venue had a mandatory tip amount that we were expected to give. It was honestly a lot lower than we thought we were going to have to tip, so I couldn't complain. Besides, the venue did an excellent job with our wedding, so they deserved every last dollar.

If you feel that your vendors just didn't do that great of a job, then don't feel pressured to tip. Regardless of what you actually end up tipping, if you do intend to leave some kind of tip, make sure to have enough cash on hand for it. You don't want the reception to end with all of your vendors having done a fantastic job, only to realize you didn't bring enough money to tip them all fairly.

I hate to admit it, but this happened to us. We didn't think ahead when it came to tipping, and our DJ did a great job, as did the photographer. But we failed to account for the fact that the DJ would have several people on his team, not just himself. The tip we gave, which was to be split among all of them, was certainly not enough for the great job that they all did. We did have some extra cash, but it was our honeymoon spending money since we were leaving the very next day to go to Asia. So long story short, bring extra cash just in case but don't feel obligated to give it all away.

And They Lived Happily Ever After

Congratulations! You finished the book! Well, either that, or you were so mind-numbingly bored with the whole subject that you decided to skip to the end. Either way, I have provided a CliffNotes outline of the material so that those of you who did read the book can refresh their memory at a glance, and those of you who skipped to the end can still get something out of this book. Bear in mind that this outline will not be as detailed as the actual chapters, but it should contain enough high-level advice to be useful.

The CliffNotes Version

1. Starting your wedding planning at least a year in advance will allow you to find the best vendors and shop around for the best prices.
2. Your wedding date will be a significant factor in your total wedding cost. In general:
   a. In the United States, weddings occurring during May through October are more expensive, with peaks occurring in June & September.
   b. Saturday is the most expensive day to have a wedding, followed by Sunday, Friday, and then all other weekdays.
   c. Daytime weddings are cheaper than evening weddings.
   d. Guest minimums will be higher for the preferred wedding dates & times.
3. Your guest count can quickly blow up once you start factoring in plus-ones, spouses, and children. You should:
   a. Divide your guests into Must-Haves and Nice-to-Haves.
   b. Further divide your Nice-To-Haves into friends and family.

c. Casually reach out to your Must-Haves to see if your tentative wedding date conflicts with anything on their schedule.
   d. Use your Must-Haves count as your minimum guest count.
4. To choose a fantastic venue for your wedding, you should:
   a. Google as many venues as you can and select at least four to visit in person.
   b. Use your Must-Haves count to guide which venues are suitable for your wedding.
   c. Compare the costs of each venue and negotiate if possible.
   d. Don't get pressured into signing just because the salesperson is pushy. Typically, this is a red flag.
5. Apply the same logic that you used to pick a venue to pick great vendors.
   a. The DJ and photographer are worth spending extra on.
   b. Whether you decide to get a videography package will depend on how well-suited your venue is for videography, as well as how romantic the story of how you met is.
   c. The florist/decorator is most definitely 100% not worth spending extra on.
   d. For the love of God, make sure to speak with your officiant about what they will say during your ceremony.
   e. There are tons of annoying requirements to get married by the Catholic Church. Just read the section about it.
   f. Transportation for you and your guests is an important but often overlooked detail. Don't forget it, but also don't overspend on this.

g. Yes, money is important. However, making sure that you pick a trustworthy vendor who makes you feel comfortable is more important.
h. Before you sign, make sure to agree on a payment schedule that works for you and be prepared to put down a sizeable deposit for your venue and each vendor.

6. After your venue and all of your vendors are booked, there will be a period of downtime. During this period, you should:
    a. Begin taking care of less time-sensitive details such as the wedding dress, wedding bands, tuxedos, honeymoon planning, save-the-dates, and invitations.
    b. During this time, you should also focus on reducing your recreational costs so that you can reallocate that money towards wedding expenses.

7. About 4 – 6 weeks before your wedding, your vendors may start contacting you to finalize all of the details. At the very latest, they should be contacting you 3 – 4 weeks before your wedding. Some things to keep in mind are:
    a. Your vendors will all be contacting you at once. This period will be stressful and will go by quicker than you think.
    b. Logistical details will need to be finalized, and final payments will need to be made. For more information regarding which aspects, in particular, will need to be finalized, you should read the section about it.
    c. Don't wait until the week of your wedding to book your rehearsal dinner venue.
    d. Whether getting married by a religious institution or a city-approved officiant, you still need to meet your state's legal requirements for marriage. Research what these requirements are and start satisfying them as soon as possible.

8. Here is some advice for your actual wedding day:
    a. Try not to stress. Easier said than done, I know. But, at this point, things are going to happen the way they happen.
    b. This day is about you and your spouse. Ignore any other drama, family-related, or otherwise, that may occur. Whatever issues arise on this day, you should face it together as it is your first challenge as a married couple.
    c. Don't forget to eat. The day will be so hectic, and you may be so busy taking pictures that you forget to eat. It's going to be a stressful enough day as it is, no need to add starvation to the pile.
    d. You will be the center of attention. Everyone is going to want a piece of you, but make sure you at least greet each of your guests.
    e. Thank your guests for coming. You will probably have little chance to actually speak with any guest at length, but when the moment comes to give a thank you speech, just make sure to have a little something prepared.
    f. Don't forget to tip your vendors. How much you tip is totally up to you, but if they did a great job and made your wedding unforgettable, they should probably be rewarded. If you do intend on tipping, make sure to account for how many people each particular vendor will be bringing so that you know how much to tip.
9. Please leave an honest review of this book!

Now, my final (I swear!) bit of advice is: This is your wedding, not your parents' wedding or any other family member's wedding for that matter. Don't let others pressure you into purchasing items or services for your wedding that you don't want. Your family should not be coercing you into picking the options that they want, especially if they are more expensive.

The exception to this, of course, is if they are footing the bill. However, as I've mentioned so many times before that my keyboard is probably worn out from typing it by now if your budget is seemingly unlimited, then this is not the book for you. And with that, I'd like to say…

Thank You for Reading! Please Share Your Feedback

Thank you all for reading this book! I sincerely hope it provided some clarity to the wedding planning process and some transparency into pricing. *The Wedding Planning Survival Guide* should be an essential tool for anybody that wants to survive the wedding planning process. Learn from my experiences and plan the shit out of your wedding!

I'd also appreciate it if you left a review sharing your honest thoughts on the content of this book. Whether you think there's room for improvement or believe that this book had everything you needed, let the world and I know! Reviews are the best way for independent authors such as myself to reach a wider audience and improve my content. Please leave your review here: https://www.amazon.com/review/create-review/?ie=UTF8&channel=glance-detail&asin=B086PMNJ19

As mentioned before, if you liked this book, and want to be the first to know when I release my next book, you should subscribe to my newsletter. I value my subscriber's feedback and will rely on them to decide what I should write about next. So, the next topic I write about could be one that you suggested! If you want to stay in the know and offer suggestions, you can subscribe here: https://www.christiansegarra.com/subscribe

Thank you all again for your time. I hope your weddings are the happiest days of your lives!

About the Author

Christian Segarra is an experienced analytics professional, having spent time in the airlines and tech industries. His hobbies include traveling, gaming, being a goofball, and learning new things. For example, he has taught himself R & Python programming, tax preparation, and how to be a semi-adequate husband. However, perhaps the hobby that brings him the most joy is finding new ways to save money... much to his wife's dismay.

Printed in Great Britain
by Amazon